# ✪ WEAPONS OF WAR
# BOMBERS AND TRANSPORT AIRCRAFT
## 1939–1945

# ✪ WEAPONS OF WAR
# BOMBERS AND TRANSPORT AIRCRAFT
## 1939–1945

CHARTWELL
BOOKS, INC.

CHARTWELL BOOKS, INC.
A division of BOOK SALES, INC.
276 Fifth Avenue Suite 206
New York, New York 10001
USA

Contributing authors: Chris Chant, Steve Crawford, Martin J. Dougherty, Ian Hogg,
Robert Jackson, Chris McNab, Michael Sharpe, Philip Trewhitt

ISBN 978-0-7858-2995-9

Printed in China

PICTURE CREDITS
Photographs: All Art-Tech/Aerospace, except page 17,
courtesy of Personal Collection/Newton Hucke.
Illustrations: © Art-Tech/Aerospace.

# CONTENTS

# Introduction

# Masters of the air

**The Allies' strategic bombing campaign proved a key factor in deciding the outcome of World War II.**

World War II started in September 1939 with the German invasion of Poland and ended in August 1945 with the American atomic bombings of the Japanese cities of Hiroshima and Nagasaki. Air power had been increasingly important throughout this period at the tactical, operational and strategic levels, but with the annihilations of Hiroshima and Nagasaki, it became clear that air power had attained a grand strategic capability and, as such, had become an arbiter of the new world order that emerged from World War II.

Many clues about the nature of the warfare that was to characterize World War II became evident in the middle and late 1930s, especially during the Italian conquest of Abyssinia (1935–36), the Spanish Civil War (1936–39), in which the Republican government was supported by the Soviet Union and the Nationalist insurgents by Germany and Italy, and the opening stages of the 2nd Sino-Japanese War (1937–45).

Over the same period there was a radical change in the technical nature of aircraft, already presaged during the late 1920s and early 1930s as fabric-covered biplanes of steel or light alloy construction were replaced in civil and then military service by monoplanes of light alloy construction covered increasingly with light alloy

**DORNIER DO 17: see page 71**

**WEAPONS OF WAR**

HEINKEL HE 111: see page 103

JUNKERS JU 52: see page 113

skinning. From about 1934, therefore, the
tactical and operational nature of the air
forces of the world's more advanced nations
was advanced by the steady development,
production and procurements of warplanes
conforming to what may be termed the
'modern' monoplane configuration. These
warplanes were typified by light alloy
construction under a covering of stressed
light alloy skinning, a cantilever low-wing
monoplane layout, landing gear in which
the main units were completely retractable,
enclosed accommodation, trailing-edge
flaps for enhanced take-off and landing
performance and propulsion by a high-
powered engine (generally an air-cooled
radial or liquid-cooled Vee unit) in a neat
low-drag cowling, driving a variable-pitch
propeller with three or more blades, cooled
by a neat radiator installation and boosted
by a mechanically driven supercharger or,
increasingly, an exhaust-driven turbocharger.

Also on the horizon, it should be
noted, was the possibility of propulsion
by reaction engines such as the rocket,
which would offer an exceptionally high
power/weight ratio, but at the same
time suffer from a prodigious specific
fuel consumption of highly dangerous
propellants. The turbojet offered a better

JUNKERS JU 87: see page 116

SM. 79 SPARVIERO: see page 157

## The full potential of air warfare against ground targets only became obvious during Germany's 'blitzkrieg' of 1939–41.

power/weight ratio than the reciprocating engine and lower specific fuel consumption than the rocket, but suffered from major development problems.

World War II began as a largely European matter with Germany's conquest of Poland in September 1939 and prompting British and French declarations of war. Between April and June 1940, the Germans turned north to overrun Denmark and Norway and, between May and June of the same year, they drove west to defeat the Netherlands, Belgium and France. This left only the UK against Germany,

which by now had been joined by Italy after the latter's declarations of war against France and the UK.

### A NEW KIND OF WAR

So far as World War II in the air proper was concerned, the increasing effectiveness of bombing and of the close support for the ground forces by bombers and fighters were indicated by the campaigns in Abyssinia and Spain during the mid-1930s, a period of transition as modern monoplane warplanes were replacing older biplanes. The full potential of air warfare

FOCKE-WULF FW 200 CONDOR: see page 92

LANCASTER: see page 35

against ground targets was first clearly demonstrated, however, in the German 'Blitzkrieg' campaigns of 1939–41. But while the Germans revealed superb tactical efficiency in these campaigns, they had not grasped the full implications of air power as a new concept of warfare, as they employed their air forces essentially in support of their land forces. Although still searching for the right air doctrine, the British were nevertheless ahead of the Germans in their overall concept of air power and it was this superiority of doctrine that combined with tactical and technical factors to give the British victory in the Battle of Britain.

Developed by the British and refined by the Americans, air doctrine had by the end of World War II reached an early

## The development of long-range bombers made it possible to carry out direct offensives against enemy industry.

definitive stage in which it comprised three closely related but still distinct major aspects: command of the air, long-range ('strategic') bombing of the enemy's war-making capabilities and direct support of surface forces (both land and sea).

Command of the air, now better known as air superiority, was vital to effective offensive employment of air assets in the other two aspects and was also significant in two defensive roles. Command of the air, or at least the ability to mount an effective challenge to enemy control of the air, was important as a means of protecting one's own economic strength

(otherwise war-making potential) against an enemy's long-range bombing and also for the protection of one's own surface forces against an enemy's air attacks. Moreover, because of the terrorizing effect that an enemy's air attacks could exert on both civil and military personnel, command of the air was a vital factor in preserving the morale of one's own side.

Command of the air could be provided by means such as defensive air combat, attrition of enemy fighter strength through repeated long-range attacks (including escort of strategic bombing that lured the

**B-17 FLYING FORTRESS: see page 47**

**WEAPONS OF WAR**

B-24 LIBERATOR: see page 70

ILYUSHIN IL-2: see page 110

WEAPONS OF WAR

MITSUBISHI G4M 'BETTY': see page 135

WEAPONS OF WAR

enemy's fighters into the air), attacks on air installations and, in the longer term, against the enemy's aircraft industry.

## STRATEGIC BOMBING

Strategic bombing had for some time been seen by air power advocates as the decisive aspect of air power. The possession of long-range bombers for the first time made feasible direct offensive operations against an enemy's war-making capability rather than indirectly by blockade. The British, despite their overall inferiority of aircraft numbers and the need to concentrate on defensive fighter capability in the early days of the war, never lost sight of offensive air warfare as their primary air objective and were undertaking long-range attacks on German industrial and commercial targets even during the Battle of Britain in 1940. However, the Germans quickly improved their fighter defence and the British were then forced to switch to night attacks, in which the prevalence of poor visual conditions and indifferent nocturnal navigational accuracy dictated an alteration from precision attacks to area bombing against major industrial regions.

## DAYLIGHT BOMBING

From a time late in 1942, US bombers, protected by armour and carrying numerous trainable guns, were able to bomb in daylight more effectively and, as a result of their use of a more effective sight, were able to strike at targets with greater

B-25 MITCHELL: see page 144

accuracy. Moreover, such bombing raids drew the German fighters into the air to face attritional combat that led to a steady reduction of German fighter strength over occupied Europe and then over Germany itself. US losses to the Germans in these daylight raids grew to alarming proportions, however, and could be continued in 1944–45 only as a result of the introduction of longer-range fighters that could escort the bombers on their raids deep into Germany.

Thus, the UK's RAF Bomber Command and the USAF's 8th and 15th Army Air Forces respectively struck at area targets by night and point targets by day. This so-called combined bomber offensive was a major force in speeding Germany's industrial and military collapse, especially after the focus for the attacks had become communications and energy producing installations, rather than specifically military targets.

Although it differed in detail, the US strategic bombing of Japan followed a course basically similar to that employed against Germany. The distances were greater, of course, which lessened the overall efficiency of the bomber offensive. However, with the capture of Iwo Jima in March 1945, US bombers and long-range fighters were able to take off from the island's two landing fields to strike at the Japanese homeland, and

SBD DAUNTLESS: see page 83

C-47 SKYTRAIN/DAKOTA: see page 80

effectively destroy the enemy's industrial infrastructure.

At the tactical level, the doctrine for close air support of ground forces reached its definitive form in World War II largely as a cooperative effort by two British formations – the Desert Air Force and the 8th Army – in North Africa during 1942. The key feature of this concept was its command arrangement, in which full control of all air units was retained by the air commander rather than ground force commanders.

This provided a flexibility in fulfilling ground force requirements and in dealing with unexpected threats that was wholly beyond systems such as that employed by the Germans, whose air units were generally assigned to ground force command. However, it must be admitted that the British system effectively prevented full integration of air support units into the land warfare team.

## THE TRIUMPH OF THE FIGHTER-BOMBER

One vital aspect of the air support doctrine was the availability of the genuine fighter-bomber. Fast and agile, this type of warplane was ideally suited to the task of delivering precise low-level bombing and strafing attacks against ground targets, but was also the only effective weapon against comparable enemy types. Thus, the first task of such fighter-bombers, assisted by light and medium bombers attacking the enemy's air installations, was to operate in the fighter role for the gaining of local air superiority, without which no other types of aircraft could undertake their tasks without heavy and possibly prohibitive losses to enemy fighters.

The role of aircraft in support of surface forces at sea was similar in concept but differed in important details. The most important revelation about the nature of maritime air power became evident right at the beginning of the war, when it was noted that the capability of bomber and torpedo aircraft against surface ships was so great that air superiority translated into surface superiority, even in situations in which the enemy had a considerable superiority in surface strength. The validity of this concept was definitely proved in the

Battle of Midway in June 1942, when the air power of a numerically inferior US force provided almost total victory over a superior Japanese force. Though the Americans lost 150 aircraft in the battle, their air arm sank four Japanese carriers, an event which marked the turning point of the sea war in the Pacific.

## THE PRIMACY OF AIR POWER

The conclusion was that carrier-borne aircraft were no longer mere supports for the surface forces but rather the primary attack element. Even the heaviest-armed and armoured battleship was vulnerable to air attack, as the sinking of the giant battleship Yamato by US aircraft in April 1945 illustrated (though it took seven bombs and 11 torpedoes to send her to the bottom).

As a result, it was quickly realized that the aircraft carrier had replaced the battleship as the capital vessel of modern warfare. Also, the aircraft carrier proved vital in its smaller forms as an escort or light carrier in the defeat – in collaboration with long-range aircraft operating from land bases – of the submarine that was the other major threat to surface vessels, both naval and mercantile. Finally, the aircraft carrier also provided tactical air support for amphibious forces landed on enemy shores.

As World War II ended, opinion about the capabilities and limitations of air power was widely divided among professional leaders, who otherwise agreed that air power had become an indispensable element of what was now a 'triphibious' combat team.

B-29 SUPERFORTRESS: see page 52

**WEAPONS OF WAR**

ARADO AR 234: see page 31

# Aichi B7A Ryusei 'Grace'

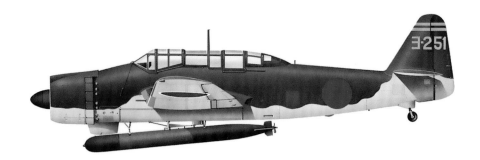

In 1941, the Imperial Japanese navy air force issued an exacting requirement for a carrierborne attack bomber to replace the Nakajima B6N torpedo bomber and Yokosuka D4Y dive-bomber. Aichi's response was the AM-23 design, and the first of nine B7A1 prototypes flew in May 1942. The development programme was constantly delayed by engine teething problems and it was April 1944 before the type: entered production as the B7A2, which offered very good handling and excellent performance. Although production in three factories was planned, only two in fact came on board and production totalled a mere 105 aircraft (80 from Aichi and 25 from the 21st Naval Air Arsenal). These had to operate from land bases as the Japanese navy had no operational aircraft carriers by this time. The aircraft pictured is a B7A2 of the Yokosuka Kokutai and is carrying a 'Long Lance' torpedo, one of the most effective weapons of its type.

## SPECIFICATIONS

**COUNTRY OF ORIGIN:** Japan
**TYPE:** (B7A2) two-seat carrierborne and land-based torpedo bomber and dive-bomber
**POWERPLANT:** one 1491kW (2000hp) Nakajima NK9C Homare 12 18-cylinder two-row radial engine
**PERFORMANCE:** maximum speed 566.5km/h (352mph); climb to 4000m (13,125ft) in 6 minutes 55 seconds; service ceiling 11,250m (36,910ft); range 3038km (1888 miles)
**WEIGHTS:** empty 3810kg (8400lb); maximum take-off 6500kg (14,330lb)
**WINGSPAN:** 14.40m (47ft 3in)
**LENGTH:** 11.49m (37ft 8in)
**HEIGHT:** 4.07m (13ft 5in)
**ARMAMENT:** two 20mm (0.79in) fixed forward-firing cannon in wing and one 13mm (0.51in) trainable rearward-firing machine gun in the rear cockpit, plus an internal bomb and torpedo load of 800kg (1764lb)

# Aichi D1A 'Susie'

In response to a 1932 requirement for an advanced carrierborne dive-bomber for the Japanese Navy, Nakajima adapted the Heinkel He 66, of which a single example had been imported from Germany with a Japanese engine to create the Aichi Special Bomber prototype. Late in 1934, the Imperial Japanese navy air force ordered Aichi to proceed with the finalization of its AB-9 design for production as the D1A1 with the 432.5kW (580hp) Nakajima Kotobuki 2 Kai 1 or Kotobuki 3 radial engine. Deliveries of this initial model totalled 162 aircraft. The company then built 428 of the improved D1A2 model with spatted wheels and an uprated engine. The D1A saw widespread service during the Sino-Japanese war, but by the time of Japan's entry into World War II in 1941, all surviving D1A1 and most D1A2 aircraft had been relegated to training units, with a mere 68 D1A2 machines operating in second-line roles until 1942.

## SPECIFICATIONS

**COUNTRY OF ORIGIN:** Japan

**TYPE:** (D1A2) two-seat carrierborne and land-based dive-bomber

**POWERPLANT:** one 544kW (730hp) Nakajima Hikari 1 nine-cylinder single-row radial engine

**PERFORMANCE:** maximum speed 309km/h (192mph); climb to 3000m (9845ft) in 7 minutes 51 seconds; service ceiling 6980m (22,900ft); range 927km (576 miles)

**WEIGHTS:** empty 1516kg (3342lb); maximum take-off 2610kg (5754lb)

**WINGSPAN:** 11.40m (37ft 5in)

**LENGTH:** 9.30m (30ft 6in)

**HEIGHT:** 3.41m (11ft 2in)

**ARMAMENT:** two 7.7mm (0.303in) fixed forward-firing machine guns in the upper part of the forward fuselage and one 7.7mm (0.303in) trainable rearward-firing machine gun in the rear cockpit, plus an external bomb load of 310kg (683lb)

# Aichi D3A 'Val'

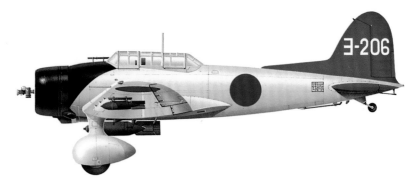

**B**est remembered as one of the two main attack types involved in the Japanese attack on Pearl Harbor in December 1941, the D3A resulted from a 1936 requirement for a D1A successor and was a trim low-wing monoplane with enclosed accommodation but fixed and nicely faired landing gear. The first of eight prototype and service trials aircraft flew in January 1938, followed by production of 470 D3A1 aircraft with the 746kW (1000hp) Mitsubishi Kinsei 43 or 898kW (1070hp) Kinsei 44 engine. It was this type that was the Japanese Navy's mainstay early in World War II. The improved D3A2 (1016 aircraft) entered service in the autumn of 1942. However, by this time the type was obsolescent and, from 1943, most of the surviving aircraft were adapted as D3A2-K trainers. Many were later used for kamikaze attacks on Allied shipping. The aircraft pictured is a D3A1 of the Yokosuka Kokota, in 1940 colours.

## SPECIFICATIONS

**COUNTRY OF ORIGIN:** Japan
**TYPE**: (D3A2) two-seat carrierborne and land-based dive-bomber
**POWERPLANT**: one 969kW (1300hp) Mitsubishi Kinsei 54 14-cylinder two-row radial engine
**PERFORMANCE:** maximum speed 430km/h (267mph); climb to 3000m (9845ft) in 5 minutes 48 seconds; service ceiling 10,500m (34,450ft); range 1352km (840 miles)
**WEIGHTS**: empty 2570kg (5666lb); maximum take-off 4122kg (9100lb)
**WINGSPAN:** 14.37m (47ft 2in)
**LENGTH:** 10.20m (33ft 5in)
**HEIGHT:** 3.8m (12ft 8in)
**ARMAMENT:** two 7.7mm (0.303in) fixed forward-firing machine guns in the upper part of the forward fuselage and one 7.7mm (0.303in) trainable rearward-firing machine gun in the rear cockpit, plus an external bomb load of 370kg (816lb)

# Aichi E13A 'Jake'

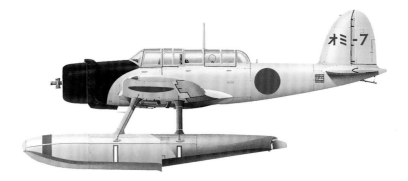

The E13A resulted from a 1937 requirement for a long-range reconnaissance floatplane and first flew in prototype: form during 1940. This paved the way for the E13A1 initial production model that entered service late in 1941. Production by three manufacturers totalled 1418 including an unknown number of prototypes and these machines were delivered in variants such as the E13A1 baseline model, E13A1-K dual-control trainer, E13A1a with detail improvements as well as exhaust flame-dampers in a nocturnal subvariant and E13A1b with air-to-surface radar. Numbers of E13A1a and E13A1b floatplanes were later adapted to the light anti-ship role with a 20mm (0.79in) cannon in a trainable downward-firing installation. The aircraft in Imperial Japanese Navy service regularly undertook patrol sorties lasting up to 15 hours, but many came to a rather ignominious end during the latter stages of the war on *kamikaze* operations.

## SPECIFICATIONS

**COUNTRY OF ORIGIN:** Japan

**TYPE:** (E13A1a) three-seat reconnaissance floatplane

**POWERPLANT:** one 805kW (1080hp) Mitsubishi Kinsei 43 14-cylinder two-row radial engine

**PERFORMANCE:** maximum speed 377km/h (234mph); climb to 3000m (9845ft) in 6 minutes 5 seconds; service ceiling 8730m (28,640ft); range 2089 km (1298 miles)

**WEIGHTS:** empty 2642kg (5825lb); maximum take-off 4000kg (8818lb)

**WINGSPAN:** 14.50m (47ft 7in)

**LENGTH:** 11.30m (37ft 1in)

**HEIGHT:** 4.70m (15ft 5in)

**ARMAMENT:** one 20mm (0.79in) trainable downward-firing cannon in the ventral position (field modification on late-production floatplanes) and one 7.7mm (0.303in) trainable rearward-firing machine gun in the rear of the cockpit, plus an external bomb load of 250kg (551lb)

# Amiot 143

First flown in April 1931, the Amiot 140 was designed to meet a 1928 requirement for a day and night bomber, long-range reconnaissance and bomber escort type. Ordered into production in November 1934 with Lorraine W-type engines, the type became the Amiot 143 with the powerplant changed to Gnome-Rhône engines. The Amiot 143M.4 entered service in 1935 and production totalled 138 aircraft, the later examples with 7.5mm (0.29in) MAC 1934 machine guns in place of the original Lewis guns, a longer nose and fixed rather than jettisonable auxiliary fuel tanks. This obsolete type still equipped six groupes de bombardement at the start of World War II but suffered heavy losses when switched from night to day operations. The surviving aircraft were operated as transports to Vichy French forces in North Africa until 1944. The aircraft pictured is a 143M, of the 3rd Escadrille of GB II/35, based at Pontarlier in September 1939.

## SPECIFICATIONS

**COUNTRY OF ORIGIN:** France
**TYPE:** (Amiot 143M.4) four/six-seat night bomber and reconnaissance warplane
**POWERPLANT:** two 640kW (870hp) Gnome-Rhône 14Kirs/Kjrs Mistral-Major 14-cylinder two-row radial engines
**PERFORMANCE:** maximum speed 310km/h (193mph); climb to 4000m (13,125ft) in 14 minutes 20 seconds; service ceiling 7900m (25,920ft); range 2000km (1243 miles)
**WEIGHTS:** empty 6100kg (13,448lb); maximum take-off 9700kg (21,385lb)
**WINGSPAN:** 24.53m (80ft 6in)
**LENGTH:** 18.26m (59ft 11in)
**HEIGHT:** 5.68m (18ft 8in)
**ARMAMENT:** up to six 7.5mm (0.29in) machine guns, plus an internal and external bomb load of 1600kg (3527lb)

# Amiot 354

Having produced the extraordinarily ungraceful Amiot 143 during the late 1920s, in the early 1930s, the Amiot design team then acquired a flair for graceful design and evolved the beautiful Amiot 341 long-range mailplane. This aircraft paved the way for the Amiot 340 bomber prototype that developed by a number of steps into the Amiot 354B.4 production bomber. The 354B.4 was one of the best aircraft of its type to enter production before World War II. Some 900 of this type were ordered and offered good performance: and potent defensive firepower. However, development and production delays meant that only about 45 had been completed before the fall of France in June 1940. The survivors were used mainly as high-speed transports, four being taken over by the Luftwaffe for clandestine operations. The aircraft pictured was the 39th delivered to the Armée de l'Air. After the war the sole surviving aircraft was operated by the French Air Ministry.

## SPECIFICATIONS

**COUNTRY OF ORIGIN:** France
**TYPE:** (Amiot 354B.4) four-seat medium bomber
**POWERPLANT:** two 1060hp (790kW) Gnome-Rhòne 14N-48/49 14-cylinder two-row radial engines
**PERFORMANCE:** maximum speed 480km/h (298mph); climb to 4000m (13,125ft) in 8 minutes 42 seconds; service ceiling 10,000m (32,810ft); range 3500km (2175 miles) with an 800kg (1764lb) bomb load
**WEIGHTS:** empty 4725kg (10,417lb); maximum take-off 11,300kg (24,912lb)
**WINGSPAN:** 22.83m (74ft 11in)
**LENGTH:** 14.50m (47ft 7in)
**HEIGHT:** 4.08m (13ft 5in)
**ARMAMENT:** one 20mm (0.79in) trainable rearward-firing cannon in the dorsal position, one 7.5mm (0.29in) trainable forward-firing machine gun in the nose and one 7.5mm (0.29in) trainable rearward-firing machine gun in a ventral mounting, plus an internal bomb load of 1200kg (2646lb)

# Arado Ar 232

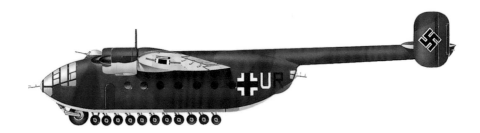

The Ar 232 was designed as a general-purpose transport with multi-wheel landing gear for operation into front-line airfields. The aircraft first flew in prototype during mid-1941 with a powerplant of two 1193kW (1600hp) BMW 801MA radial engines. The design incorporated innovative features with provision for easy loading into and unloading from the pod-like main section of the fuselage. BMW 801 engines were required more urgently for combat aircraft, such as the Focke Wulf 190, and the third prototype introduced the powerplant of four BMW Bramo 323 radial engines on the leading edges of a centre section of increased span. This basic configuration was retained for the 19 or so Ar 232B production aircraft that were completed (one of them fitted with captured French Gnome-Rhòne engines) for intensive service between 1942 and 1945. Most of these aircraft served with KG 200, the Luftwaffe's special operations unit.

## SPECIFICATIONS

**COUNTRY OF ORIGIN:** Germany
**TYPE:** (Ar 232B-0) four-seat medium transport
**POWERPLANT:** four 895kW (1200hp) BMW Bramo 323R-2 Fafnir nine-cylinder single-row radial engines
**PERFORMANCE:** maximum speed 340km/h (211mph); climb to 4000m (13,125ft) in 15 minutes 48 seconds; service ceiling 6900m (22,640ft); range 1335km (830 miles)
**WEIGHTS:** empty 12,800kg (28,219lb); maximum take-off 21,160kg (46,649lb)
**WINGSPAN:** 33.50m (109ft 11in)
**LENGTH:** 23.52m (77ft 2in)
**HEIGHT:** 5.70m (18ft 8in)
**ARMAMENT:** one 20mm (0.79in) trainable cannon in the dorsal turret, one 13mm (0.51in) trainable forward-firing machine gun in the nose position and one or two 13mm (0.51in) trainable rearward/downward-firing machine guns in the rear of the fuselage pod

# Arado Ar 234B Blitz

The wheeled trolley/skid used in the Ar 234 prototypes for take-off and landing was clearly impractical for an operational aeroplane, so plans for the Ar 234A production derivative of the Ar 234 V3 were dropped in favour of the Ar 234B. This utilized tricycle landing gear in which all three units retracted into the fuselage, an arrangement pioneered in the Ar 234 V9. The Ar 234B was intended for the reconnaissance bomber role with hardpoints under the fuselage and two engine nacelles for bombs up to 1102lb (500kg) weight. Some 20 Ar 234B-0 pre-production aircraft were followed by 210 Ar 234B-1 reconnaissance aircraft with drop tanks in place of bombs and Ar 234B-2 reconnaissance bombers. The type entered service in September 1944, and the Ar 234B was complemented by just 14 examples of the Ar 234C with the revised powerplant of four 1764lb st (7.85kN) BMW 109-003A-1 turbojets.

## SPECIFICATIONS

**COUNTRY OF ORIGIN:** Germany
**TYPE:** (Ar 234B-2) single-seat reconnaissance bomber
**POWERPLANT:** two 8.825kN (1984lb) Junkers Jumo 109-004B-1/2/3 Orkan turbojet engines and provision for two 4.90kN( 1102lb) Walter HWK 109-500 (R I-202b) RATO units
**PERFORMANCE:** maximum speed 742km/h (461mph); climb to 6000m (19,685ft) in 12 minutes 48 seconds with a 500kg (1102lb) bomb load; service ceiling 10,000m (32,810ft); range 1630km (1013 miles)
**WEIGHTS:** empty 5200kg (11,464lb); maximum take-off 9850kg (21,715lb)
**WINGSPAN:** 14.11m (46ft 4in)
**LENGTH:** 12.64m (41ft 6in)
**HEIGHT:** 4.30m (14ft 1in)
**ARMAMENT:** two 20mm (0.79in) fixed rearward-firing cannon in the underside of the rear fuselage and an external bomb load of 1500kg (3307lb)

# Armstrong Whitworth Albemarle

The Albemarle medium bomber was designed by Bristol during 1939, but production was transferred to Armstrong Whitworth when it became clear that the latter had spare design and production capacity. Subsequently the Albemarle was redesigned as a reconnaissance bomber with an airframe of steel and wood (thereby reducing demand on strategic light alloys) that could be produced largely by subcontractors for assembly on a single line. The first of two prototypes flew in March 1940, and was a poor performer as a result of its great structural weight. Production of 600 aircraft was then undertaken in the revised airborne forces support role for service from January 1943 as the first British operational aeroplane with tricycle landing gear. The Mks I, II and VI differed only in details and were completed as paratroop transports and glider tugs, while the Mk V was only a glider tug.

## SPECIFICATIONS

**COUNTRY OF ORIGIN:** United Kingdom
**TYPE:** (Albemarle Mk II) three-seat paratroop transport and glider tug
**POWERPLANT:** two 1186kW (1590hp) Bristol Hercules XI 14-cylinder two-row radial engine
**PERFORMANCE:** maximum speed 426km/h (265mph); initial climb rate 279m (980ft) per minute; service ceiling 5485m (18,000ft); range 2092km (1300 miles)
**WEIGHTS:** empty 11,497kg (25,347lb); maximum take-off 16,556kg (36,500lb)
**WINGSPAN:** 23.47m (77ft)
**LENGTH:** 18.26m (59ft 11in)
**HEIGHT:** 4.75m (15ft 7in)
**ARMAMENT:** two 7.7mm (0.303in) trainable machine guns in the dorsal position

# Armstrong Whitworth Whitley

Obsolescent at the beginning of World War II, the Whitley was nonetheless one of Bomber Command's mainstays in 1939 and enjoyed an important role in the early days of the war as a night bomber before passing to Coastal Command as a patrol and anti-submarine type, ending its days as a glider-towing and paratroop training machine. The Whitley Mk I (34 aircraft) entered service in March 1937 with Armstrong Siddeley Tiger radial engines, which were retained in the 126 improved Mk II and Mk III aircraft, while the 33 Whitley Mk IV bombers switched to Rolls-Royce Merlin engines and introduced a powered tail turret. The main variant was the Mk V with a longer rear fuselage, revised tail unit and greater fuel capacity and these 1466 aircraft were followed by the 146 Mk VII aircraft for Coastal Command with air-to-surface search radar. The aircraft pictured wears pre-war insignia and was operated by No 10 Squadron, RAF, from Dishworth in 1937.

## SPECIFICATIONS

**COUNTRY OF ORIGIN:** United Kingdom
**TYPE:** (Whitley Mk V) five-man long-range night bomber
**POWERPLANT:** two 854kW (1145hp) Rolls-Royce Merlin X 12-cylinder Vee engines
**PERFORMANCE:** maximum speed 370km/h (230mph); climb to 4570m (15,000ft) in 16 minutes; service ceiling 7925m (26,000ft); range 2655km (1650 miles) with standard fuel and a 1361kg (3000lb) bomb load
**WEIGHTS:** empty 8777kg (19,350lb); maximum take-off 15,195kg (33,500lb)
**WINGSPAN:** 25.60m (84ft)
**LENGTH:** 21.49m (70ft 6in)
**HEIGHT:** 4.57m (15ft)
**ARMAMENT:** one 7.7mm (0.303in) trainable forward-firing machine gun in the nose turret, and four 7.7mm (0.303in) trainable rearward-firing machine guns in the tail turret, plus an internal bomb load of 7000lb (3175kg)

# Avro Lancaster B.Mk I (Special)

**A**fter it had gained experience with the accurate delivery of single Deep Penetration-type bombs with the 5443kg (12,000lb) 'Tallboy' (of which 854 were dropped in anger), the Royal Air Force agreed to undertake missions with the heaviest weapon of this class, the 9979kg (22,000lb) 'Grand Slam'. This was designed to penetrate deep into the earth before detonating, thus creating an earthquake effect. The bomber designed to carry this weapon from March 1945 was the Lancaster B.Mk I (Special), of which 33 were built by converting Lancaster B.Mk I aircraft with a lengthened and doorless bomb bay and, to save weight, no nose or dorsal turrets. The aircraft were operated by No.617 Squadron, which dropped 41 such bombs, with considerable success, on U-boat pens and transportation chokepoints. This unusual colour scheme was worn by one of the aircraft of the squadron's C Flight. Note the retaining chain under the bomb.

## SPECIFICATIONS

**COUNTRY OF ORIGIN:** United Kingdom
**TYPE:** Lancaster B.Mk I [Special] five-seat special mission bomber
**POWERPLANT:** four 1223kW (1640hp) Rolls-Royce Merlin 24 12-cylinder Vee engines
**PERFORMANCE:** maximum speed 462km/h (287mph); initial climb rate 76m (250ft) per minute; service ceiling 5790m (19,000ft); range 2494km (1550 miles) with a 9979kg (22,000lb) bomb load
**WEIGHTS:** empty 16,083kg (35,457lb); maximum take-off 32,659kg (72,000lb)
**WINGSPAN:** 31.09m (102ft)
**LENGTH:** 21.18m (69ft 6in)
**HEIGHT:** 6.25m (20ft 6in)
**ARMAMENT:** four 7.7mm (0.303in) trainable machine guns in the tail turret, plus a semi-internal bomb load of one 9979kg (22,000lb) 'Grand Slam' bomb

# Avro Lancaster Mk I

The most successful and celebrated heavy night bomber used by the Royal Air Force in World War II, the Lancaster was a development of the Manchester with the revised powerplant of four Rolls-Royce Merlin Vee engines. The Lancaster first flew on 9 January 1941 and entered service from the beginning of 1942. The original Lancaster Mk I soon developed an enviable reputation as a sturdy aeroplane that handled well in the air, possessed moderately good performance and had good defensive and offensive firepower. The fact that the type was essentially 'right' from its beginning is indicated in that few changes were made other than minor engine and equipment details in the course of a long production run that saw the delivery of 7378 aircraft including 3294 examples of the Lancaster Mk I (later Lancaster B.Mk I and finally B.Mk X). Pictured is a Lancaster Mk 1 of No 463 Squadron, RAF, based at Waddington in spring 1945.

## SPECIFICATIONS

**COUNTRY OF ORIGIN:** United Kingdom
**TYPE:** (Lancaster Mk I) seven-seat heavy night bomber
**POWERPLANT:** four 1223kW (1640hp) Rolls-Royce Merlin XX, 22 or 24 12-cylinder Vee engines
**PERFORMANCE:** maximum speed 462km/h (287mph); initial climb rate 76m (250ft) per minute; service ceiling 5790m (19,000ft); range 2784km (1730 miles) with a 5443kg (12,000lb) bomb load
**WEIGHTS:** empty 16,783kg (37,000lb); maximum take-off 29,484kg (65,000lb)
**WINGSPAN:** 31.09m (102ft)
**LENGTH:** 21.18m (69ft 6in)
**HEIGHT:** 6.25m (20ft 6in)
**ARMAMENT:** two 7.7mm (0.303in) trainable machine guns in the nose turret, two 7.7mm (0.303in) trainable machine guns in the dorsal turret, four 7.7mm (0.303in) trainable machine guns in the tail turret and provision for one 7.7mm (0.303in) trainable machine gun in a ventral turret, plus an internal bomb load of 8165kg (18,000lb)

# Avro Lancaster Mk I (Special)

In 1943, the British decided that a major blow could be struck at Germany's war-making industries by the destruction of the dams controlling the rivers through the Ruhr industrial region. This decision led to one of the most celebrated bombing raids of the war, using 'bouncing' bombs that were spun backward, then released at precise height, speed and distance from the target dam to skip over the water, hit the rear face of the dam and then sink down the face before exploding with devastating force. No. 617 Squadron was created for the task and, on 17 May 1943, this unit flew 19 converted Lancaster B.Mk Is to attack five of the dams, of which three were breached for the loss of eight aircraft. The raid was an enormous morale-booster to the British, but did not achieve the strategic results anticipated. Note the serial ED912/G on the aircraft pictured, which indicates a special aircraft that must be kept under armed guard when on the ground.

## SPECIFICATIONS

**COUNTRY OF ORIGIN:** United Kingdom
**TYPE:** (Lancaster Mk I Special) six-seat special mission bomber
**POWERPLANT:** four 1223kW (1640hp) Rolls-Royce Merlin 24 12-cylinder Vee engines
**PERFORMANCE:** maximum speed 462km/h (287mph); initial climb rate 76m (250ft) per minute; service ceiling 5790m (19,000ft ); range 2784km (1730 miles) with a 5443kg (12,000lb) bomb load
**WEIGHTS:** empty 16,783kg (37,000lb); maximum take-off 29,484kg (65,000lb)
**WINGSPAN:** 31.09m (102ft)
**LENGTH:** 21.18m (69ft 6in)
**HEIGHT:** 6.25m (20ft 6in)
**ARMAMENT:** two 7.7mm (0.303in) trainable machine guns in the nose turret, four 7.7mm (0.303in) trainable machine guns in the tail turret and one 7.7mm (0.303in) trainable machine gun in the ventral position, plus a 3900kg (8599lb) 'bouncing bomb' semi-recessed under the fuselage

# Lancaster Mk III and Mk X

**W**hen it became clear that production by Rolls-Royce of its great Merlin engine would not be able to keep pace with the manufacture of the airframes designed to use it, the decision was made to use the American licence-built version, namely the Packard V-1650 in its Merlin 28, 38 or 224 forms. When this engine was installed in the Lancaster Mk I, the aeroplane was known as the Lancaster Mk III (later B.Mk III and finally B.Mk 3), and deliveries of this model totalled 3020 aircraft. The Lancaster Mk III was also selected for production in Canada by Victory Aircraft Ltd. of Toronto, which delivered 430 examples of the Lancaster Mk X (later B.Mk X and finally B.Mk 10) that were identical in all important respects to the Mk III machines. KB861 was one of a batch of 300 aircraft built as Lancaster Mk Xs by Victory Aircraft, with Packard engines and the Martin 250-CE23 electrically driven mid-upper turret with 12.7mm (0.5in) guns.

## SPECIFICATIONS

**COUNTRY OF ORIGIN:** United Kingdom
**TYPE:** (Lancaster Mk III) seven-seat heavy night bomber
**POWERPLANT:** four 1223kW (1640hp) Packard (Rolls-Royce) Merlin 28, 38 or 224 12-cylinder Vee engines
**PERFORMANCE:** maximum speed 462km/h(287mph); initial climb rate 76m (250ft) (1730 miles) with a 5443kg (12,000lb) bomb load
**WEIGHTS:** empty 16,783kg (37,000lb); maximum take-off 29,484kg (65,000lb)
**WINGSPAN:** 31.09m (102ft)
**LENGTH:** 21.18m (69ft 6in)
**HEIGHT:** 6.25m (20ft 6in)
**ARMAMENT:** two 7.7mm (0.303in) trainable machine guns in the nose, turret, two 7.7mm (0.303in) trainable machine guns in the dorsal turret and four 7.7mm (0.303in) trainable machine guns in the tail turret, plus an internal bomb load of 8165kg (18,000lb)

# Avro Lancaster Mk VI

To perform the role of electronic countermeasures and electronic counter-countermeasures for the Pathfinder Force, a total of nine Lancaster bombers were converted from Mk 1 and Mk III aircraft, (two and nine respectively). These were re-engined with the two-stage supercharged Merlin 85/87 in circular cowlings (with curved ventral radiator) that were later used on Lincolns and Shackletons. With four-bladed paddle propellors the Mk VI had tremendous performance, especially as all armament except the tail turret was removed. One was logged at 555km/h (345mph). The Mk VI also benefited from an improved version of the H2S bombing radar; the main antenna for this unit was protected by a ventral fairing. This example served with No 635 Squadron, a dedicated Pathfinder unit. To identify aircraft operating in the Pathfinder role the fins were painted with high-visibility stripes, as can be seen above.

## SPECIFICATIONS

**COUNTRY OF ORIGIN:** United Kingdom
**TYPE:** seven-seat heavy night bomber
**POWERPLANT:** four 1223kW (1640hp) Packard Merlin 85/87 12-cylinder Vee engines
**PERFORMANCE:** maximum speed 555km/h (345mph); initial climb rate 76m (250ft) per minute; service ceiling 6500m (21,418ft); range 2494km (1550 miles) with a 9979kg (22,000lb) bomb load
**WEIGHTS:** empty 16,083kg (35,457lb); maximum take-off 32,659kg (72,000lb)
**WINGSPAN:** span 31.09m (102ft)
**LENGTH:** 21.18m (69ft 6in)
**HEIGHT:** 6.25m (20ft 6in)
**ARMAMENT:** four 7.7mm (0.303in) trainable machine guns in the tail turret

# Avro Manchester

**B**y the mid-1930s. the steady improvement in aeronautical design allowed the Air Ministry to plan a new generation of advanced medium bombers and, in 1936, issued a requirement that elicited responses from both Avro and Handley Page. Both companies received prototype orders, although the Handley Page did not progress beyond the drawing board. The Avro type was the Manchester medium bomber that first flew in July 1939 after the initial order for 200 aircraft had been built. The Manchester Mk I became operational in November 1940 and these 20 aircraft were followed by 180 examples of the Manchester Mk IA with larger endplate vertical surfaces on the tail, allowing the removal of the Mk I's centreline surface. The Manchester had an ideal airframe, but was rendered a failure by its wholly unreliable Vulture engines and finally retired in June 1942. Pictured is a Mk 1 of No 207 Squadron, RAF Bomber Command in early 1941.

## SPECIFICATIONS

**COUNTRY OF ORIGIN:** United Kingdom
**TYPE:** (Manchester Mk I) seven-seat medium bomber
**POWERPLANT:** two 1312kW (1760hp) Rolls-Royce Vulture I 24-cylinder X-type engines
**PERFORMANCE:** maximum speed 426km/h (265mph); service ceiling 5850m (19,200ft); range 2623km (1630 miles) with 3674kg (8100lb) of bombs
**WEIGHTS:** empty 13,350kg (29,432lb); maximum take-off 25,402kg (56,000lb)
**WINGSPAN:** 27.46m (90ft 1in)
**LENGTH:** 21.14m (69ft 4in)
**HEIGHT:** 5.94m (19ft 6in)
**ARMAMENT:** two 7.7mm (0.303in) trainable forward-firing machine guns in the nose turret, two 7.7mm (0.303in) trainable machine guns in a ventral turret later replaced by a dorsal turret and four 7.7in (0.303in) trainable rearward-firing machine guns in the tail turret, plus an internal bomb load

# Blackburn Baffin

After the Finnish Air Force had replaced the Napier Lion W-type engine with a radial engine in most of its licence-built Blackburn Ripon torpedo bombers, Blackburn followed a similar course to create the two T.5J (Ripon Mk V) private-venture prototypes. These aircraft were then redesigned as the B-4 and B-5 with 485kW (650hp) Armstrong Siddeley Tiger I and 406kW (545hp) Bristol Pegasus IMS radial engines respectively. The prototypes flew in 1932 and there followed two Pegasus IM3-powered T.8 pre-production aircraft. These paved the way for the Baffin Mk I, of which 97 were delivered up to June 1935 in the form of 38 and 30 Ripon Mk IIA and Mk IIC conversions, as well as 29 new-build aircraft. The Baffin was declared obsolete in September 1937, which allowed New Zealand to buy 19 aircraft for coastal patrol service up to 1942. Pictured is one of the B-5 aircraft operated by the Finnish Air Force.

## SPECIFICATIONS

**COUNTRY OF ORIGIN:** United Kingdom
**TYPE:** (Baffin Mk I) two-seat carrierborne and land-based torpedo and level bomber
**POWERPLANT:** one 421kW (565hp) Bristol Pegasus IM3 nine-cylinder single-row radial engine
**PERFORMANCE:** maximum speed 219km/h (136mph); initial climb rate 146m (480ft) per minute; service ceiling 4570m (15,000ft); range 869km (450 miles)
**WEIGHTS:** empty 1452kg (3200lb); maximum take-off 3452kg (7610lb)
**WINGSPAN:** 13.88m (45ft 7in)
**LENGTH:** 11.68m (38ft 4in)
**HEIGHT:** 3.91m (12ft 10in)
**ARMAMENT:** one 7.7mm (0.303in) fixed forward-firing machine gun in the upper port side of the forward fuselage and one 7.7mm (0.303in) trainable rearward-firing machine gun in the rear cockpit, plus an external torpedo and bomb load of 907kg (2000lb)

# Blackburn Botha

**D**esigned to meet a 1935 requirement for a twin-engined reconnaissance bomber with a bomb bay large enough to accommodate an 457mm (18in) torpedo, the Botha first flew in prototype form during December 1938. Trials revealed that the type had a number of handling problems and was also seriously underpowered, but the handling problems were cured and the type was placed in production (580 aircraft) with the option of marginally uprated engines. The first aircraft to be delivered to the RAF was the third aircraft off the Dumbarton production line, which arrived at No 12 Maintenance Unit, Kemble, in December 1939. Entering service in May 1940, the Botha proved so inadequate for coastal reconnaissance and attack purposes that only two operational squadrons converted to the type, which was soon relegated to second-line duties. The Botha survived as a navigation and gunnery trainer into 1944 and was unsuccessful even in this secondary role.

## SPECIFICATIONS

**COUNTRY OF ORIGIN:** United Kingdom

**TYPE:** (Botha Mk I) four-seat reconnaissance and torpedo bomber used mainly for training and communications

**PERFORMANCE:** two 694kW (930hp) Bristol Perseus XA nine-cylinder single-row radial engine

**PERFORMANCE:** maximum speed 401km/h (249mph); initial climb rate 300m (985ft) per minute; service ceiling 5610m (18,400ft); range 2044km (1270 miles)

**WEIGHTS:** empty 5366kg (11,830lb); maximum take-off 8369kg (18,450lb)

**WINGSPAN:** 17.98m (59ft)

**LENGTH:** 15.56m (51ft 1in)

**HEIGHT:** 4.46m (14ft 8in)

**ARMAMENT:** one 7.7mm (0.303in) fixed forward-firing machine gun in the nose and two 7.7mm (0.303in) trainable machine guns in the dorsal turret, plus an internal bomb and torpedo load of 907kg (2000lb)

# Bloch MB.174

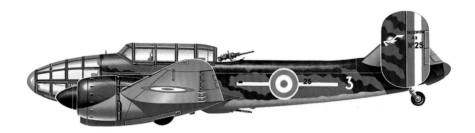

The origins of the Bloch MB.174 can be traced to a time late in 1936, when Bloch began to plan the MB.170 multi-role warplane that could be operated in the A.3 three-seat army co-operation or AB.2 two-seat attack bomber roles. The MB.170 first flew in February 1938, and the type: was eventually ordered as the MB.174, primarily for reconnaissance and target-marking operations but with light bombing as a secondary role. The MB.174A.3 retained the flying surfaces, landing gear and powerplant: of the MB.170B.3 in combination with a redesigned fuselage. The cockpit was moved farther to the rear and the nose received a fair measure of glazing. Only 56 of this model were completed and played a modest part in the defensive campaign that preceded France's capitulation in June 1940. Pictured is one of the aircraft operated by Groupe de Reconnaissance II/33 during the Battle of France. Some were later used by the Vichy Air Force.

## SPECIFICATIONS

**COUNTRY OF ORIGIN:** France
**TYPE:** (MB.174A.3) three-seat light reconnaissance bomber
**POWERPLANT:** two 850kW (1140hp) Gnome-Rhône 14N-48/49 14-cylinder two-row radial engines
**PERFORMANCE:** maximum speed 530km/h (329mph); climb to 8000m (26,250ft) in 11 minutes; service ceiling 11,000m (36,090ft); range 1285km (798 miles) with an 400kg (882lb) bomb load
**WEIGHTS:** empty 5600kg (12,346lb); maximum take-off 7160kg (15,784lb)
**WINGSPAN:** 17.90m (58ft 9in)
**LENGTH:** 12.25m (40ft 2in)
**HEIGHT:** 3.55m (11ft 8in)
**ARMAMENT:** two 7.5mm (0.29in) fixed forward-firing machine guns in the leading edges of the wing, two 7.5mm (0.29in) trainable rearward-firing machine guns in the dorsal position and three 7.5mm (0.29in) rearward-firing machine guns in the ventral position, plus an internal bomb load of 400kg (882lb)

# Bloch MB.200

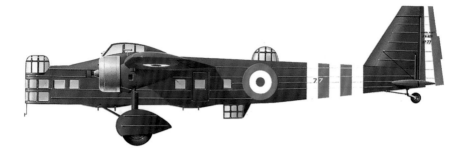

**D**esigned to replace the obsolete Liorè-et-Olivier LeO 20 in the night bomber role, the Bloch MB.200 was typical of the highly angular French warplanes of the late 1920s and early 1930s and first flew in MB.200.01 prototype form in June 1933. An initial 30 MB.200B.4 bombers were ordered in December of the same year and the type entered service in 1934. Eventual French production by six companies – Bloch, Breguet, Hanriot, Loire, Potez and SNCASO – was 208 aircraft and another 124 aircraft were built under licence in Czechoslovakia by the Aero and Avia companies. The type was obsolete by 1939 and most French aircraft were soon relegated to the training role. Many continued in service after France's defeat. A number of the aircraft were expropriated by the Germans for their own use and transfer to allies. Pictured is one of the aircraft operated by Section de Remorquage d'Orange in May 1940.

## SPECIFICATIONS

**COUNTRY OF ORIGIN:** France
**TYPE:** (MB.200B.4) four-seat medium bomber
**POWERPLANT:** two 649kW (870hp) Gnome-Rhòne 14Kirs/Kjrs Mistral-Major 14- cylinder two-row radial engines
**PERFORMANCE:** maximum speed 283km/h (176mph); climb to 4000m (13,125ft) in 13 minutes; service ceiling 8000m (26,245ft); range 1000km (621 miles)
**WEIGHTS:** empty 4300kg (9840lb); maximum take-off 7480kg (16,490lb)
**WINGSPAN:** 22.45m (73ft 7.88in)
**LENGTH:** 15.80m (51ft 10in)
**HEIGHT:** 3.92m (12ft 10in)
**ARMAMENT:** one 7.5mm (0.29in) trainable forward-firing machine gun in the nose turret, one 7.5mm (0.29in) trainable machine gun in the dorsal turret and one 7.5mm (0.29in) trainable rearward-firing machine gun in the ventral gondola, plus an external bomb load of 1200kg (2646lb)

# Blohm und Voss Bv 138

The Bv 138 was projected and built in prototype form as the Ha 138, with three Junkers Jumo 205D Diesel engines, before undergoing a virtually total redesign in 1938, the year in which the Hamburger Flugzeugbau was absorbed fully into Blohm und Voss. The first of six Bv 138A-0 pre-production flying boats made its maiden flight in February 1939. These machines were followed by 25 Bv 138A-1 production boats with three 447kW (600hp) Jumo 205C-4 engines. The type saw its first operational service in April 1940. Six and 14 Bv 138B-0 and B-1 machines introduced a strengthened structure and greater power respectively, while the definitive Bv 138C-1 (about 227 boats) had more strengthening and better defensive armament. The designation Bv 138MS was used for minesweeper conversions. Pictured here is a BV 138C-1 of 2/KüF/Gr. 406, based in northern Norway in March 1942.

## SPECIFICATIONS

**COUNTRY OF ORIGIN:** Germany
**TYPE:** (Bv 138C-1) five-seat maritime reconnaissance flying boat
**POWERPLANT:** three 746kW (1000hp) Junkers Jumo 205D 12-cylinder vertically opposed Diesel engines
**PERFORMANCE:** maximum speed 285km/h (177mph); climb to 3000m (9845ft) in 22 minutes 48 seconds; ceiling 5000m (16,405ft); range 4300km (2672 miles)
**WEIGHTS:** empty 11,770kg (25,948lb); maximum take-off 17,650kg (38,912lb)
**WINGSPAN:** 26.94m (88ft 5in)
**LENGTH:** 19.85m (65ft 2in)
**HEIGHT:** 5.90m (19ft 4in)
**ARMAMENT:** one 20mm (0.79in) trainable forward-firing cannon in the bow turret, one 20mm (0.79in) trainable rearward-firing cannon in the rear-hull turret, one 13mm (0.51in) trainable rearward-firing machine gun behind the central engine nacelle and one 7.92mm (0.31in) trainable lateral-firing machine gun in starboard hull position, plus a bomb load of 300kg (661lb)

# Blohm und Voss Bv 141

**D**esigned as a tactical reconnaissance aeroplane to the same requirement as the Focke-Wulf Fw 189, the Bv 141 had a highly unusual asymmetric layout with the fully glazed crew nacelle offset to starboard of the centreline and a boom (carrying the engine at its front and a tail unit at its rear) offset to port. The first of three prototypes flew in February 1938, and there followed five Bv 141A-0 pre-production aircraft. The type had poor performance as a result of its use of the 645kW (865hp) BMW 132N engine, so the next five aircraft were redesigned Bv 141B-0 machines with an uprated powerplant as well as a strengthened structure and a revised tail unit. These aircraft were used for operational trials over the UK and the Soviet Union from the autumn of 1941, but there were development delays and the programme was ended in 1943. Depicted is one of the pre-production aircraft (BV 141A-04), as evaluated by the Luftwaffe at the Erprobungstelle factory in late 1939.

## SPECIFICATIONS

**COUNTRY OF ORIGIN:** Germany
**TYPE:** (Bv 141B-0) three-seat tactical reconnaissance and observation aeroplane with limited close support capability
**POWERPLANT:** one 1163kW (1560hp) BMW 801A 14-cylinder two-row radial engine
**PERFORMANCE:** maximum speed 438km/h (272mph); initial climb rate not available; service ceiling 10,000m (32,810ft); range 1900km (1181 miles)
**WEIGHTS:** empty 4700kg (10,362lb); maximum take-off 6100kg (13,448lb)
**WINGSPAN:** 17.46m (57ft 4in)
**LENGTH:** 13.95m (45ft 9in)
**HEIGHT:** 3.60m (11ft 10in)
**ARMAMENT:** two 7.92mm (0.31in) fixed forward-firing machine guns in the front of the crew nacelle, one 7.92mm (0.31in) trainable rearward-firing machine gun in the dorsal position and one 7.92mm (0.31in) trainable rearward-firing machine gun in the rotating tailcone position, plus an external bomb load of 200kg (441lb)

# Blohm und Voss Bv 222 Wiking

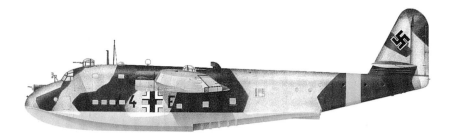

The Wiking (Viking) started life as a 1937 project for a 24-passenger flying boat airliner to operate between Berlin and New York. The type was then revised as a long-range maritime reconnaissance type and was the largest flying boat to enter operational service in World War II. There were eight prototypes, the first of them flying in September 1940. The Bv 222B was the unrealized civil model and the military version was planned as the Bv 222C, of which only four Bv 222C-0 pre-production examples were completed. The prototypes entered transport service in mid-1941, mainly in the Mediterranean and, from 1943, were revised for the reconnaissance role and supplemented by the four pre-production boats. The boats then served over the Atlantic, Baltic and Arctic regions. Only four boats survived to the end of the war. One of these was flown to RAF Calshot for evaluation and later equipped No 201 Squadron.

## SPECIFICATIONS

**COUNTRY OF ORIGIN:** Germany
**TYPE:** (Bv 222C) transport and maritime reconnaissance flying boat
**POWERPLANT:** six 746kW (1000hp) Junkers Jumo 207C 12-cylinder vertically opposed Diesel engines
**PERFORMANCE:** maximum speed 390km/h (242mph); initial climb rate 144m (473ft) per minute; ceiling 7300m (23,950ft); range 6100 km (3790 miles)
**WEIGHTS:** empty 30,650kg (67,572lb); maximum take-off 49,000kg (108,025lb)
**WINGSPAN:** 46m (150ft 11in)
**LENGTH:** 37m (121ft 5in)
**HEIGHT:** 10.90m (35ft 9in)
**ARMAMENT:** one 20mm (0.79in) trainable cannon in the dorsal turret, one 20mm (0.79in) trainable cannon in each of the two power-operated wing turrets, one 13mm (0.51in) trainable forward-firing machine gun in the bow position and one 13mm (0.51in) trainable lateral-firing machine gun in each of the four lateral hull positions

# Boeing B-17C Flying Fortress

The Model 299 was designed to meet a 1934 requirement for a multi-engined medium bomber and envisaged primarily for the coast-defence role. The aircraft first flew as a private-venture prototype: with provision for a 2177kg (4800lb) bomb load and was later evaluated as the XB-17. Orders were then placed for 14 YB-17 and YB-17A service test aircraft that were later accepted as B-17 and B-17A aircraft, and paved the way for the 39 B-17B aircraft with a modified nose, 38 B-17B aircraft with greater power and defensive armament, and 42 B-17D aircraft with an additional crew member. Some 20 B-17Cs were transferred to the UK as Fortress Mk I machines; most of the B-17D bombers were stationed in the Far East, where about half were destroyed by Japan's pre-emptive attacks of 7 December 7 1941. Note the ventral bathtub and flush waist positions on the B-17C illustrated here. The B-17C was the fastest of all versions, with a maximum speed of 515km/h (320mph).

## SPECIFICATIONS

**COUNTRY OF ORIGIN:** United States
**TYPE:** (B-17C) nine-seat medium bomber
**POWERPLANT:** four 895kW (1200hp) Wright R-1820-65 nine-cylinder single-row radial engines
**PERFORMANCE:** maximum speed 515km/h (320 mph); climb to 3050m (10,000ft) in 7 minutes 30 seconds; service ceiling 11,280m (37,000ft); range 5471km (3400 miles)
**WEIGHTS:** empty 13,880kg (30,600lb); maximum take-off 22,521kg (49,650lb)
**WINGSPAN:** 31.62m (103ft 9in)
**LENGTH:** 20.70m (67ft 11in)
**HEIGHT:** 4.70m (15ft 5in)
**ARMAMENT:** two 7.5mm (0.29in) forward-firing machine guns in cheek positions, three 12.7mm (0.5in) machine guns in dorsal positions, two 12.7mm (0.5in) machine guns in the ventral position and one 12.7mm (0.5in) machine gun in each of the two waist positions, plus an internal bomb load of 4761kg (10,496lb)

# Boeing B-17G Flying Fortress

The B-17G Flying Fortress resulted directly from the experience of the US bomber crews in 1943, which revealed that the B-17F lacked adequate defence against head-on fighter attack. The primary change in the B-17G was therefore the introduction of a power-operated chin turret armed with two 12.7mm (0.5in) machine guns, which were controlled remotely from the glazed nose position. This proved to be a more practical unit as it lost the one or two manually operated 12.7mm (0.5in) machine guns that had been fitted in the B-17F. Deliveries began in September 1943. A number of other operational improvements were steadily incorporated during the production of 8680 aircraft from three manufacturers in the period up to April 1945. The B-17G was the cornerstone of the US Army Air Forces' bomber effort in Europe during 1944 and 1945. The aircraft pictured is the famed B-17G *A Bit o'Lace* of the 711th BS, 447th BG, based at Rattlesden.

## SPECIFICATIONS

**COUNTRY OF ORIGIN:** United States
**TYPE:** (B-17G) 10-seat heavy bomber
**POWERPLANT:** four 895kW (1200hp) Wright R-1820-97 nine-cylinder radial engines
**PERFORMANCE:** maximum speed 486km/h (302mph); climb to 6095m (20,000ft) in 37 minutes; service ceiling 10,850m (35,600ft); range 2897km (1800 miles)
**WEIGHTS:** empty 20,212kg (44,560lb); maximum take-off 32,659kg (72,000lb)
**WINGSPAN:** 31.63m (103ft 9in)

**LENGTH:** 22.78m (74ft 9in)
**HEIGHT:** 5.82m (19ft 1in)
**ARMAMENT:** two 12.7mm (0.5in) machine guns in chin turret, one 12.7mm (0.5in) machine gun in each cheek position, two 12.7mm (0.5in) trainable machine guns in dorsal turret, one 12.7mm (0.5in) machine gun in roof position, two 12.7mm (0.5in) machine guns in ventral turret, one 12.7mm (0.5in) machine gun in each waist position, two 12.7mm (0.5in) machine guns in tail, plus a bomb load of 7983kg (17,600lb)

# Boeing B-17F Flying Fortress

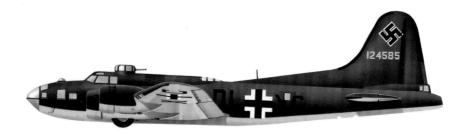

The B-17D paved the way for the first large-scale production model of the Flying Fortress, the B-17E. Some 512 were delivered and featured a wholly redesigned and enlarged tail unit for improved stability at high altitude, and a completely revised defensive scheme including a twin-gun tail position and power-operated twin-gun dorsal and ventral turrets. The B-17E entered service in 1942, and was soon supplemented by the B-17F. This was the definitive model, as indicated by a production total of 3405 aircraft from three manufacturers. The B-17F introduced a frameless Plexiglas nose transparency, structural strengthening for higher-weight operations, and further refinement of the defensive armament. Small numbers of B-17E and B-17F bombers were operated by the British with the designations Fortress Mk IIA and Fortress Mk II respectively. A number were captured intact by the Germans and evaluated in Luftwaffe markings.

## SPECIFICATIONS

**COUNTRY OF ORIGIN:** United States
**TYPE:** (B-17F) 10-seat medium bomber
**POWERPLANT:** four 895kW (1200hp) Wright R-1820-97 nine-cylinder single-row radial engines
**PERFORMANCE:** maximum speed 523km/h (325mph); climb to 6095m (20,000ft) in 25 minutes 42 seconds; ceiling 11,430m (37,500ft); range 7113km (4420 miles)
**WEIGHTS:** empty 16,206kg (35,728lb); maximum take-off 32,6591kg (72,000lb)
**WINGSPAN:** 31.63m (103ft 9in)
**LENGTH:** 22.78m (74ft 9in)
**HEIGHT:** 5.85m (19ft 3in)
**ARMAMENT:** two 7.62mm (0.3in) trainable forward-firing machine guns in cheek positions, three 12.7mm (0.5in) trainable machine guns in dorsal positions, two 12.7mm (0.5in) trainable machine guns in the ventral position and one 12.7mm (0.5in) trainable lateral-firing machine gun in each of the two waist positions, plus an internal bomb load of 4761kg (10,496lb)

# Boeing B-29

The Boeing B-29 made a highly significant contribution to the Allied war effort, quite out of proportion with its length of service. Although most aircraft were completed as heavy bombers, many were later modified for different tasks such as air/sea rescue, turbojet research or air refuelling. In 1942 Boeing began development of a transport version of the Boeing B-29 with a large upper lobe to create a 'double bubble' fuselage. This was designated Model 367 and first flew in November 1944. Together with Consolidated C-87s and modified B-24s, the B-29 was pressed into service as a tanker to bring to Chinese airfields the fuel needed for missions over Japan. Many were permanently modified as tankers, an example being B-29-1-BW- 42-6242 Esso Express, one of the first production block, which served with the 486th BG. This aircraft is painted in early olive-drab camouflage; later aircraft were unpainted to reduce drag.

## SPECIFICATIONS

**COUNTRY OF ORIGIN:** United States
**TYPE**: (B-29) nine-seat long-range heavy bomber
**POWERPLANT**: four 1640kW (2200hp) Wright R-3350-23 18-cylinder two-row radial engines
**PERFORMANCE**: maximum speed 576km/h (358mph); climb to 6095m (20,000ft) in 38 minutes; service ceiling 9710m (31,850ft); range 9382km (5830 miles)
**WEIGHTS**: empty 31,816kg (70,140lb); normal take-off 47,628kg (105,000lb); maximum take-off 56,246kg (124,000lb)
**WINGSPAN**: 43.05m (141ft 3in)
**LENGTH**: 30.18m (99ft)
**HEIGHT**: 9.02m (29ft 7in)
**ARMAMENT**: one 20mm (0.79in) trainable rearward-firing cannon and two 12.7mm (0.5in) trainable rearward-firing machine guns in the tail position, plus an internal bomb load of 9072kg (20,000lb)

# Boeing B-29A Superfortress

The B-29 is generally remembered as the warplane which, on 6 and 9 August 1945, dropped atomic weapons that destroyed the cities of Hiroshima and Nagasaki, persuading the Japanese to surrender. Yet by this time the B-29 had been at the forefront of a campaign to neutralize the war-making potential of Japan by burning her cities, destroying her communications network and crippling her industries. First entering service from the summer of 1944, the Superfortress was an extremely clean bomber with turbocharged engines. The baseline B-29, of which 2458 were completed, was complemented by the B-29A, of which 1119 were manufactured, with greater span and a four- rather than two-gun forward dorsal barbette, plus the B-29B of which 310 were delivered with reduced defensive armament, but a greater bomb load and higher speed. The aircraft pictured was allocated to the 500th Bomb Group of the 73rd Bomb Wing.

## SPECIFICATIONS

**COUNTRY OF ORIGIN:** United States
**TYPE:** (B-29) nine-seat long-range heavy bomber
**POWERPLANT:** four 1640kW (2200hp) Wright R-3350-23 18-cylinder two-row radial engines
**PERFORMANCE:** maximum speed 576km/h (358mph); climb to 6095m (20,000ft) in 38 minutes; service ceiling 9710m (31,850ft); range 9382km (5830 miles)
**WEIGHTS:** empty 31,816kg (70,140lb); normal take-off 47,628kg (105,000lb); maximum take-off 56,246kg (124,000lb)
**WINGSPAN:** 43.05m (141ft 3in)
**LENGTH:** 30.18m (99ft)
**HEIGHT:** 9.02m (29ft 7in)
**ARMAMENT:** one 20mm (0.79in) trainable rearward-firing cannon and two 12.7mm (0.5in) trainable rearward-firing machine guns in the tail position and two 12.7mm (0.5in) trainable machine guns in each of two dorsal and two ventral barbettes, plus an internal bomb load of 9072kg (20,000lb)

# Breda Ba.88 Lince

First flown in October 1936, the Lince (Lynx) proved fiercer in name than deed. The type set a number of records during development, however, the addition of military equipment added weight and drag, which resulted in wholly inadequate performance and degraded handling, despite the adoption of an uprated powerplant and two, rather than one, vertical tail surfaces. The first 88 aircraft were completed between May and October 1939. In the first phase of the North African campaign, the aircraft proved tactically useless, and the survivors were soon being used as decoys for attacking British warplanes. By this time 155 aircraft had been made, but most of the new aircraft were scrapped. The designation Ba 88M was used for three aircraft converted in 1943 as dive-bombers with a lengthened wing, downrated powerplant and revised armament. Pictured is a Ba 88 of the 7th Gruppo, 5th Stormo da Combattimento, based in Libya in 1940.

## SPECIFICATIONS

**COUNTRY OF ORIGIN:** Italy

**TYPE:** two-seat ground-attack warplane

**POWERPLANT:** two 746kW (1000hp) Piaggio P.XI RC.40 14-cylinder two-row radial piston engines

**PERFORMANCE:** maximum speed 490km/h (304mph); climb to 3000m (9845ft) in 7 minutes 30 seconds; service ceiling 8000m (26,245ft); range 1640km (1020 miles)

**WEIGHTS:** empty 4650kg (10,252lb); maximum take-off 6750kg (14,881lb)

**WINGSPAN:** 15.60m (51ft 2in)

**LENGTH:** 10.79m (35ft 5in)

**HEIGHT:** 3.10m (10ft 3in)

**ARMAMENT:** three 12.7mm (0.5in) fixed forward-firing machine guns and one 7.7mm (0.3in) trainable rearward-firing machine gun, plus an internal bomb load of 1000kg (2205lb)

# Breguet Bre.521 Bizerte

After buying a single example of the Short S.8 Calcutta flying boat from the UK and building four more under licence with the designation S.8/2, Breguet developed its own version as the Bre.521 Bizerte. This first flew in prototype form during September 1933, and was followed by three pre-production boats and then 27 boats to the full production standard with an uprated powerplant and other improvements. The Bre.521Hy.8 entered service late in 1935 and, at the start of World War II, the French had 20 boats in service with four squadrons of the French naval air service. After the defeat of France the surviving boats were entrusted to two Vichy French units and, when in November 1942 the Germans occupied Vichy France, they seized eight Bizertes for continued use in the air/sea rescue role. One is seen here in the colours of 1.Seentostaffel of the Luftwaffe, based at Brest-Hourtin in north west France in winter of 1943–44.

## SPECIFICATIONS

**COUNTRY OF ORIGIN:** France
**TYPE:** (Bre.521Hy.8) eight-seat maritime reconnaissance and bomber flying boat
**POWERPLANT:** three 671kW (900hp) Gnome-Rhône 14Kirs-1 Mistral-Major 14-cylinder two-row radial engines
**PERFORMANCE:** maximum speed 243km/h (151mph); climb to 2000m (6560ft) in 8 minutes 46 seconds; service ceiling 6000m (19,685ft); range 3000km (1864 miles)
**WEIGHTS:** empty 9470kg (20,878lb); maximum take-off 16,600kg (36,597lb)
**WINGSPAN:** 35.15m (115ft 4in)
**LENGTH:** 20.48m (67ft 2in)
**HEIGHT:** 7.48m (24ft 7in)
**ARMAMENT:** five 7.5mm (0.29in) trainable machine guns mounted singly in the tail position, two port and starboard forward positions and two port and starboard waist positions, plus external bomb load of 300kg (661lb)

# Breguet Bre.695

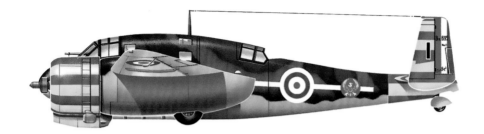

**W**orried about the strategic danger to the country as a result of its limited aero engine manufacturing capability, France decided in 1939 to adopt a policy of ensuring that every major warplane type in French service would be capable of accepting an imported American or British engine. This led to the Bre.695.01, which was the Bre.690.01 prototype revised with two Pratt & Whitney R-1830-SB4G Twin Wasp radial engines. These were of lighter weight and greater power than the French engines they replaced, but also of larger diameter. The Bre.695.01 first flew in March 1940 and, while flight trials confirmed the overall viability of the revised powerplant, they also revealed a number of problems. Even so, large-scale orders for the Bre.695AB.2 were planned, but only 50 had been completed before France's defeat in June 1940. Pictured is a Breguet 695 AB.2 of the 1e Escadrille, GBA I/151 of the Armée de l'Air de l'Armistice, based at Lézignan-Corbières in June 1942.

## SPECIFICATIONS

**COUNTRY OF ORIGIN:** France
**TYPE:** two-seat light attack bomber
**POWERPLANT:** two 640.5kW (825hp) Pratt & Whitney R-1830-SB4G Twin Wasp 14-cylinder two-row radial engines
**PERFORMANCE:** maximum speed 560km/h (348mph); service ceiling 9000m (29,530ft); range 1500km (932 miles)
**WEIGHTS:** maximum take-off 5400kg (11,905lb)
**WINGSPAN:** 15.36m (50ft 5in)
**LENGTH:** 9.67m (31ft 9in)
**HEIGHT** 3.19m (10ft 6in)
**ARMAMENT:** one 20mm (0.79in) fixed forward-firing cannon and two 7.5mm (0.29in) fixed forward-firing machine guns, one 7.5mm (0.29in) fixed obliquely rearward- firing machine gun, two 7.5mm (0.29in) fixed obliquely downward/ rearward-firing machine guns and one 7.5mm (0.29in) trainable rearward-firing machine gun, plus an internal bomb load of 400kg (882lb)

# Beaufighter Mks X and XI

The Beaufighter TF.Mk X was an improved version of the Beaufighter Mk VIC with Hercules XVII engines optimized for the low- rather than medium-altitude as required for anti-shipping operations. An AI.Mk VIII radar was fitted in a 'thimble' nose for use in tracking surface vessels, a dorsal gun provided defensive fire and provision was made for underwing bomb and rocket loads as alternatives to the underfuselage torpedo. The combination of a large dorsal fin and enlarged elevators improved control at high weights. Production of the Beaufighter TF.Mk X, which was the most important British anti-ship attack weapon from 1944 in Europe and the Far East, totalled 2205 aircraft, and another 163 machines were completed to the Beaufighter Mk XIC standard that differed from the Beaufighter TF.Mk X only in that it possessed no torpedo capability. The aircraft pictured is a TF. Mk X of No 455 Squadron, RAF.

## SPECIFICATIONS

**COUNTRY OF ORIGIN:** United Kingdom
**TYPE:** (Beaufighter TF.Mk X) two/three-seat anti-ship attack fighter
**POWERPLANT:** two 1320kW (1770hp) Bristol Hercules XVII 14-cylinder two-row radial engines
**PERFORMANCE:** maximum speed 512km/h (318mph); climb to 1525m (5000ft) in 3 minutes 30 seconds; service ceiling 4570m (15,000ft); range 2913km (1810 miles)
**WEIGHTS:** empty 7076kg (15,600lb); maximum take-off 11,431kg (25,200lb)
**WINGSPAN:** 17.63m (57ft 10in)
**LENGTH:** 12.70m (41ft 8in)
**HEIGHT:** 4.83m (15ft 10in)
**ARMAMENT:** four 20mm (0.79in) fixed forward-firing cannon in the underside of the forward fuselage and one 7.7mm (0.303in) trainable rearward-firing machine gun in the dorsal position, plus an external torpedo, bomb and rocket load of 1111kg (2450lb)

# Bristol Beaufighter Mk 21

The Royal Australian Air Force evinced an interest in the Beaufighter from an early stage. Reliable twin-engined powerplant, heavy firepower and good overall performance (especially in range) were attractive to a force facing the possibility of Japanese attack on the north coast of Australia, a region that was both inhospitable and lacking in a network of closely spaced airfields. As a result, the Department of Aircraft Production commenced building the Beaufighter TF.Mk X as the Beaufighter TF.Mk 21 with two Hercules XVIII engines rated for optimum performance at medium altitude. Other changes included removal of the torpedo shackles, the radar and the dorsal fin fillet, modification of the wing for four 12.7mm (0.5in) machine guns and addition of a bulge in the nose for a Sperry autopilot that was in fact seldom fitted. The first of 364 such aircraft flew in May 1944. The aircraft pictured wears the colours of No 22 Squadron, RAAF.

## SPECIFICATIONS

**COUNTRY OF ORIGIN:** Australia
**TYPE:** (Beaufighter Mk 21) two/three-seat multi-role heavy fighter
**POWERPLANT:** two 1320kW (1770hp) Bristol Hercules XVIII 14-cylinder two-row radial engines
**PERFORMANCE:** maximum speed 512km/h (318mph); climb to 1525m (5000ft) in 3 minutes 30 seconds; service ceiling 4570m (15,000ft); range 2913km (1810 miles )
**WEIGHTS:** empty 7076kg (15,600lb); maximum take-off 11,431kg (25,200lb)
**WINGSPAN:** 17.63m (57ft 10in)
**LENGTH:** 12.70m (41ft 8in)
**HEIGHT:** 4.83m (15ft 10in)
**ARMAMENT:** four 20mm (0.79in) fixed forward-firing cannon in forward fuselage, four 12.7mm (0.5in) fixed forward-firing machine guns in the leading edges of the wing and one 7.7mm (0.303in) rearward-firing machine gun in the dorsal position, plus an external bomb and rocket load of 2450lb (1111kg)

# Bristol Bombay

**A**s first flown in June 1935, the Bombay was a comparatively simple high-wing monoplane with fixed tailwheel landing gear and resulted from a 1931 requirement for dual-role transport and bomber optimized for service in Africa, the Middle East and India. Thus the new type had to be able to carry 24 troops or an equivalent weight of freight (including items as large as an aero engine), be fitted with defensive armament and possess the capability for service as a bomber with an externally carried bomb load. Orders were placed for 50 production aircraft and these entered service in March 1939, by which time they were technically obsolete. Even so, the aircraft performed valuable service in the North African and Mediterranean theatres as transports and were also used at times as bombers. The survivors were retired mid-way through World War II. Shown here in the colours of No. 216 Squadron, RAF, based in Egypt in 1940–41, is a Bombay Mk 1.

## SPECIFICATIONS

**COUNTRY OF ORIGIN:** United Kingdom
**TYPE:** (Bombay Mk I) three/six-seat transport and bomber
**POWERPLANT:** two 753kW (1010hp) Bristol Pegasus XXII nine-cylinder radial engines
**PERFORMANCE:** maximum speed 309km/h (192mph); climb to 4570m (15,000ft) in 20 minutes; service ceiling 7620m (25,000ft); range 2230 miles (3589km)
**WEIGHTS:** empty 6260kg (13,800lb); maximum take-off 9072kg (20,000lb)
**WINGSPAN:** 29.18m (95ft 9in)
**LENGTH:** 21.11m (69ft 3in)
**HEIGHT:** 5.94m (19ft 6in)
**ARMAMENT:** one 7.7mm (0.303in) trainable forward-firing machine gun in nose turret and one 7.7mm (0.303in) trainable rearward-firing machine gun in tail turret; option of one 7.7mm (0.303in) trainable machine gun in each of two beam positions, plus a bomb load of 907kg (2000lb)

# Bristol Blenheim Mk IV

The Blenheim Mk IV was designed to overcome the operational deficiencies of the Blenheim Mk I. It differed in its uprated powerplant and significantly increased fuel capacity. Another revsion was the forward fuselage, which was lengthened by some 0.91m (3ft) to include a navigator's station under a glazed upper surface with a downward-scalloped port side. The Blenheim Mk IV entered production early in 1939 and, by the outbreak of war, the RAF had 13 squadrons of Mk IVs. British production by three companies (Bristol, Avro and Rootes) totalled 3285. Finland also produced 10 aircraft for its own use and 676 aircraft were produced in Canada with the name Bolingbroke. The Blenheim Mk IV bomber equipped 25, 19 and one squadrons in the UK, Middle East and Far East respectively and numbers of the aircraft were later converted to Blenheim Mk IVF night-fighter standard with a ventral gun pack and radar.

## SPECIFICATIONS

**COUNTRY OF ORIGIN:** United Kingdom
**TYPE:** (Blenheim Mk IV) three-seat light bomber
**POWERPLANT:** two 742kW (995hp) Bristol Mercury XV nine-cylinder single-row radial engines
**PERFORMANCE:** maximum speed 428km/h (266mph); initial climb rate 457m (1500ft) per minute; service ceiling 6705m (22,000ft); range 2350km (1460 miles) with a 454kg (1000lb) bomb load
**WEIGHTS:** empty 4456kg (9823lb); maximum take-off 6804kg (15,000lb)
**WINGSPAN:** 17.17m (56ft 4in)
**LENGTH:** 12.98m (42ft 7in)
**HEIGHT:** 3.90m (12ft 10in)
**ARMAMENT:** one 7.7mm (0.303in) fixed forward-firing machine gun in the leading edge of the port wing, two 7.7mm (0.303in) trainable machine guns in the dorsal turret and two 7.7mm (0.303in) trainable rearward-firing machine guns in undernose blister position, plus internal bomb load of 454kg (1000lb)

# Bristol Blenheim Mk V

The Blenheim Mk V (originally Bisley Mk I) was a final attempt to wring improved performance out of the Bristol Type 142 airframe. It was schemed in 1940 as a low-level bomber with the possibility of development into a low-level fighter and dual-control trainer. The two-seat Blenheim Mk V was basically the Blenheim Mk IV with a revised forward fuselage (including a fixed forward-firing armament of four 7.7mm (0.303in) machine guns in its port side), an improved windscreen, some 272kg (600lb) of external armour protection, a dorsal turret with a gyro sight and engines optimized for medium-altitude operations. Production eventually totalled 942 aircraft to the Mk V bomber, Mk VA ground-attack, Mk VB operational trainer and Mk VD tropicalized Mk VA standards. The type: entered service in North Africa during November 1942, but served mainly with Far East squadrons. Poor performance prompted their withdrawal after only nine months of service.

## SPECIFICATIONS

**COUNTRY OF ORIGIN:** United Kingdom
**TYPE:** (Blenheim Mk VA) three/two-seat light bomber
**POWERPLANT:** two 708kW (950hp) Bristol Mercury XXX nine-cylinder single-row radial engines
**PERFORMANCE:** maximum speed 418km/h (260mph); service ceiling 9450m (31,000ft); range 2575km (1600 miles)
**WEIGHTS:** empty 4990kg (11,000lb); maximum take-off 7711kg (17,000lb)
**WINGSPAN:** 17.17m (56ft 4in)
**LENGTH:** 13.39m (43ft 11in)
**HEIGHT:** 3.90m (12ft 10in)
**ARMAMENT:** two 7.7mm (0.303in) trainable machine guns in the dorsal turret and two 7.7mm (0.303in) trainable rearward-firing machine guns in the undernose blister position, plus an internal bomb load of 454kg (1000lb)

# CANT Z.501 Gabbiano

The first Gabbiano (Seagull) made its maiden flight in 1934 and gave notice of its capabilities by establishing a world seaplane distance record of 4955km (3080 miles) between Trieste and Berbera in British Somaliland. Production for the Italian air force started in 1936, with some 202 boats of this type in service when Italy entered World War II in June 1940. Operational experience in the maritime reconnaissance role soon revealed that the Z.501 lacked the performance and defensive firepower for successful operation against fighter opposition, resulting in the type's relegation to the air/sea rescue and coastal patrol tasks. Even so, production continued to the middle of 1943 and resulted in the overall delivery of 444 boats including small numbers delivered to Romania and Nationalist Spain. Pictured is one of the aircraft operated by 2 Escuadrilla, Grupo 62, Agrupacion Espanola (Spanish nationalist air force), based in Majorca in 1939.

## SPECIFICATIONS

**COUNTRY OF ORIGIN:** Italy
**TYPE:** (Z.501) five-seat maritime reconnaissance and bomber flying boat
**POWERPLANT:** one 671kW (900hp) Isotta-Fraschini Asso XI R2C.15 12-cylinder Vee engine
**PERFORMANCE:** maximum speed 275km/h (171mph); climb to 4000m (13,125ft) in 16 minutes; service ceiling 7000m (22,965ft); range 2400km (1491miles)
**WEIGHTS:** empty 3840kg (8466lb); maximum take-off 7050kg (15,542lb)
**WINGSPAN:** 22.50m (73ft 10in)
**LENGTH:** 14.30m (46ft 11in)
**HEIGHT:** 4.40m (14ft 6in)
**ARMAMENT:** one 7.7mm (0.3in) trainable forward-firing machine gun in the bow position, one 7.7mm (0.3in) trainable machine gun in the nacelle turret and one 7.7mm (0.3in) trainable rearward-firing machine gun in the dorsal turret, plus an external bomb load of 640kg (1411lb)

# CANT Z.506 Airone

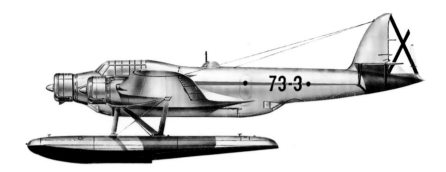

The Z.506 was derived from the Z.505 prototype that was planned as a mailplane to connect Italy with its East Africa colonies, which lacked major airfields. The aircraft was subsequently placed in production as a 15-passenger civil transport (20 aircraft) before production switched to the Z.506B Airone (heron) military derivative that entered service in 1938. Production of the Z.506B totalled some 324 aircraft, of which 95 were in service at the time of Italy's entry into World War II. The type was initially operated in the bomber role, but was then revised with stronger defensive armament and reassigned to the maritime reconnaissance, convoy escort and anti-submarine roles. A number of aircraft were also converted to the Z.506S standard for the air/sea rescue task, many of which were retained in service up to 1959. Illustrated here is a Z.506B wearing the colours of Grupo 73, Agrupacion Espanola, based at Majorca in 1939.

## SPECIFICATIONS

**COUNTRY OF ORIGIN:** Italy
**TYPE:** (Z.506B) five-seat maritime reconnaissance and bomber floatplane
**POWERPLANT:** three 559kW (750hp) Alfa Romeo 126 RC.34 nine-cylinder single-row radial engines
**PERFORMANCE:** maximum speed 350km/h (217mph); climb to 4000m (13,125ft) in 20 minutes; service ceiling 8000m (26,245ft); range 1705 miles (2745 km)
**WEIGHTS:** empty 8300kg (18,298lb); maximum take-off 12,705kg (28,008lb)
**WINGSPAN:** 26.50m (86ft 11in)
**LENGTH:** 19.24m (63ft 2in)
**HEIGHT:** 7.45m (24ft 6in)
**ARMAMENT:** one 12.7mm (0.5in) trainable machine gun in the dorsal turret, one 7.7mm (0.3in) trainable rearward-firing machine gun in the rear of the ventral gondola and one 7.7mm (0.3in) trainable lateral-firing machine gun in each of the two lateral positions, plus an internal bomb load of 1200kg (2646lb)

# CANT Z.1007 Alcione

First flown in prototype form during March 1937, the Z.1007 Alcione (Kingfisher) entered service late in 1938 and became one of Italy's most important medium bombers. Production totalled only about 35 aircraft with 626kW (840hp) Piaggio Asso XI radial engines and a defensive armament of four 7.7mm (0.3in) machine guns. This initial variant was followed by 526 examples of the Z.1007bis and Z.1007ter. The former introduced a larger airframe, an uprated powerplant with engines in revised nacelles and different armament, as well as two types of tail unit (single vertical surface in the first three batches and twin surfaces in the last six batches). The latter had the uprated powerplant of three 876kW (1175hp) Piaggio P.XIX radial engines, but a reduced 1000kg (2205lb) bomb load. This aircraft has the markings of the Aviazione Nazionale Republicana, the air force formed in 1943 from the Regia Aeronautica.

## SPECIFICATIONS

**COUNTRY OF ORIGIN:** Italy
**TYPE:** (Z.1007bis) five-seat medium bomber
**POWERPLANT:** three 746kW (1000hp) Piaggio P.XI R2C.40 14-cylinder two-row radial engines
**PERFORMANCE:** maximum speed 466km/h (290mph); climb to 4000m (13,125ft) in 10 minutes 30 seconds; service ceiling 8200m (26,900ft); range 1750km (1087 miles) with a 1200kg (2646lb) bomb load
**WEIGHTS:** empty 9396kg (20,715lb); maximum take-off 13,621kg (30,029lb)
**WINGSPAN:** 24.80m (81ft 4in)
**LENGTH:** 18.35mn (60ft 3in)
**HEIGHT:** 5.22m (17ft 5in)
**ARMAMENT:** one 12.7mm (0.5in) trainable machine gun in the dorsal turret, one 12.7mm (0.5in) trainable rearward-firing machine gun in the ventral step position and one 7.7mm (0.3in) lateral-firing machine gun in each of the two beam positions, plus an internal bomb load of 1200kg (2646lb)

# Caproni Bergamaschi Ca.135

Intended as a fast medium bomber of modern concept, the Ca.135 proved a major disappointment to the Italians. The prototype first flew in April 1935 and the Italian Air Force ordered 14 Ca.135 tipo Spagna aircraft for operational evaluation in the Spanish Civil War. In the event, deliveries were made too late for this to happen. Some 32 generally similar Ca.135 tipo Peru bombers were delivered to the Peruvian Air Force. After evaluation of two Ca.135 tipo Spagna aircraft revised with two 746kW (1000hp) Fiat A.80 RC.41 radial engines, which proved unreliable, the main production model was the Ca.135/P.XI with Piaggio radial engines. About 100 of these aircraft were completed for delivery to the Hungarian Air Force, which relegated the survivors from the operational to the training role in the second half of 1942. One of these aircraft is depicted here, wearing recognition markings indicative of service in southern Russia.

## SPECIFICATIONS

**COUNTRY OF ORIGIN:** Italy

**TYPE:** (Ca 135/P.XI) four-seat medium bomber

**POWERPLANT:** two 746kW (1000hp) Piaggio P.XI RC.40 14-cylinder two-row radial engines

**PERFORMANCE:** maximum speed 440km/h (273mph); climb to 5000m (16,405ft) in 17 minutes 24 seconds; service ceiling 6500m (21,325ft); range 1200km (746 miles) with a 1600kg (3527lb) bomb load

**WEIGHTS:** empty 6050kg (13,340lb); maximum take-off 9550kg (21,050lb)

**WINGSPAN:** 18.80m (61ft 8in)

**LENGTH:** 14.40m (47ft 3in)

**HEIGHT:** 3.40m (11ft 2in)

**ARMAMENT:** one 12.7mm (0.5in) trainable forward-firing machine gun in the nose turret, one 12.7mm (0.5in) trainable machine gun in the dorsal turret and one 12.7mm (0.5in) trainable machine gun in the ventral turret, plus an internal bomb load of 1600kg (3527lb)

# Caproni Bergamasca Ca.310 Libeccio

**A** close relative of the Ca.308 Borea civil transport and Ca.309 Ghibli multi-role colonial warplane (with fixed undercarriage), the Ca.310 Libeccio (South-west Wind) was the first of a major series of attack, bomber, reconnaissance, torpedo and trainer aircraft with retractable landing gear. The Ca.310 first flew in prototype form during April 1937 and entered limited Italian service in 1938, when 16 aircraft were sent to Spain for operational trials. Caproni was more successful in the export market, soon capturing orders from Hungary, Norway, Peru and Yugoslavia. Not all the aircraft were delivered after the customers found that performance was well below that which had been promised and 33 aircraft returned by Hungary were taken onto Italian Air Force strength as temporary replacements for the unsatisfactory Breda Ba 65. Pictured is a Ca.103M of the 8a Escuadrilla, Grupo num 18, Agrupacion Espanola in Spain during late 1938.

## SPECIFICATIONS

**COUNTRY OF ORIGIN:** Italy
**TYPE:** (Ca 310) three-seat light reconnaissance bomber
**POWERPLANT:** two 350.5kW (470hp) Piaggio P.VII C.35 seven-cylinder single-row radial engines
**PERFORMANCE:** maximum speed 365km/h (227mph); climb to 4000m (13,125ft) in 12 minutes 23 seconds; service ceiling 7000m (22,965ft); range 1200km (746 miles)
**WEIGHTS:** empty 3040kg (6702lb); maximum take-off 4650kg (10,251lb)
**WINGSPAN:** 16.20m (53ft 2in)
**LENGTH:** 12.20m (40ft)
**HEIGHT:** 3.52m (11ft 7in)
**ARMAMENT:** two 7.7mm (0.303in) fixed forward-firing machine guns in the leading edges of the wing and one 7.7mm (0.303in) trainable machine gun in the dorsal turret, plus an internal bomb load of 400kg (882lb)

# Caproni Ca.101

In 1927, Caproni introduced the Ca.101 transport as an enlarged tri-motor development of the Ca 97 transport that was produced with one, two and three engines. The type was soon ordered by the Italian Air Force as a bomber with three 276kW (370hp) Piaggio P.VII radial engines. The Ca.101 did not remain in Italian metropolitan service for long and, after their relegation from this primary role, the aircraft were revised for dual-role bomber and transport service in Italy's East African colony of Eritrea with less powerful, but more reliable and economical Alfa Romeo Dux or D.2 radial engines. Some 20 aircraft were sold to Hungary, which operated them on the Eastern Front against the Soviet Union, phasing the aircraft out of service only at the start of 1943. Pictured is a Ca.101 of the C./III Bombázó Osztály, Magyar Királyi Légierö (Royal Hungarian air force), based at Papa in Hungary, early in 1941.

## SPECIFICATIONS

**COUNTRY OF ORIGIN:** Italy

**TYPE:** (Ca.101) three-seat light reconnaissance bomber

**POWERPLANT:** three 179kW (240hp) Alfa Romeo D.2 nine-cylinder single-row radial engines

**PERFORMANCE:** maximum speed 165km/h (103mph); climb to 5000m (16,405ft) in 40 minutes 30 seconds; ceiling 6100m (20,015ft); range 2000km (1243 miles)

**WEIGHTS:** empty 3275kg (7221lb); maximum take-off 4975kg (10,968lb)

**WINGSPAN:** 19.68m (64ft 7in)

**LENGTH:** 14.37m(47ft 2in)

**HEIGHT:** 3.89m (12ft 9in)

**ARMAMENT:** one 7.7mm (0.303in) trainable machine gun in the dorsal position, one or two 7.7mm (0.303in) trainable rearward-firing machine guns in the ventral  position and, on some aircraft, one 7.7mm (0.303in) trainable lateral-firing machine guns in each of the one or two beam positions, plus an internal and external bomb load 500kg (1102lb)

# Caproni Ca.133

An improved version of the Ca.101 dual-role bomber and transport, the Ca.133 introduced a number of drag-lowering features, namely neat long-chord cowlings (housing three uprated engines), together with faired legs and spatted wheels for the main landing gear units, an improved tail unit and split flaps on the wing trailing edges. The Italian Air Force soon realized that, despite its improvements, the type was suitable only for colonial use in North and East Africa. Ca.133 production totalled 419 aircraft and conversions included 21 Ca.133S air ambulances and 329 Ca.133T pure transports with reduced defensive armament. The Ca.133 during heavy losses at the hands of British fighters after Italy's entry into World War II in June 1940. A small batch of Ca.133 aircraft was also exported to Austria in the mid-1930s. Pictured is one of the aircraft operated by Bomberstaffel 1B, Fliegerregiment Nr 2 of the Austrian air force, based at Zeltwig in 1937.

## SPECIFICATIONS

**COUNTRY OF ORIGIN:** Italy
**TYPE:** (Ca 133) three-seat bomber and transport
**POWERPLANT:** three 343kW (460hp) Piaggio Stella P.VII C.16 seven-cylinder single-row radial engines
**PERFORMANCE:** maximum speed 265km/h (165mph); service ceiling 5500m (18,045ft); range 1350km (838 miles)
**WEIGHTS:** empty 4190kg (9237lb); maximum take-off 6700kg (14,771lb)
**WINGSPAN:** 21.24m (68ft 8in)
**LENGTH:** 15.36m (50ft 5in)
**HEIGHT:** 4m (13ft 1in)
**ARMAMENT:** one 7.7mm (0.303in) trainable machine gun in the dorsal position, two 7.7mm (0.3in) trainable rearward-firing machine guns in the ventral position and one 7.7mm (0.303in) trainable lateral-firing machine gun in the door on the port side of the fuselage, plus an external bomb load of 1200kg (2646lb)

# Caproni Ca.148

ALA LITTORIA

I-ETIO

The Ca.148 was the last development of the Ca.101 and appeared in 1938 as an 18-passenger transport with a powerplant of three 343kW (460hp) Piaggio Stella P.VII RC radial engines, each driving a three-blade metal propeller of the variable-pitch type. The cockpit was moved forward by 0.60m (2ft) from its original location under the wing leading edge, the fuselage door was relocated from its original position under the port wing root trailing edge to a position farther to the rear and the landing gear was strengthened to cater for an increased maximum take-off weight. Production totalled 106 aircraft intended mainly for civil and military operation in East Africa, but a number of the aircraft were operated as military transports by the Germans and the Italians in the European theatre. Some Ca.148s remained in Italian service until the late 1940s. Ca.148 I-ETIO of the Italian airline Ala Littoria (pictured here) saw service during the Abyssinian campaign.

## SPECIFICATIONS

**COUNTRY OF ORIGIN:** Italy
**TYPE:** (Ca 148) two-seat transport with accommodation for 18 troops
**POWERPLANT:** three 343kW (460hp) Piaggio Stella P.VII C.16 seven-cylinder single-row radial engines
**PERFORMANCE:** maximum speed 265km/h (165mph); service ceiling 5500m (18,045ft); range 1350km (838 miles)
**WEIGHTS:** empty 4190kg (9237lb); normal take-off 4970kg (10,596lb)
**WINGSPAN:** 21.24m (68ft 8in)
**LENGTH:** 15.36m (50ft 5in)
**HEIGHT:** 4m (13ft 1in)
**ARMAMENT:** none

# Caudron C.445 Goéland

**D**esigned as an advanced monoplane to capture a slice of the emerging feederliner and executive transport market, the Goéland (seagull) first flew in 1934 as the C.440 and entered production with two 164kW (220hp) Renault Bengali-Six engines. These were replaced in the C.441 with identically rated Renault 6Q-01 engines. The C.441 also introduced a modified wing that was retained in the C.444 (with Renault 6Q-00/01 engines) and then the C.445 with increased outer wing dihedral. The C.445 entered civil and military service. The French Air Force ordered the C.445M for the light transport, communications and crew training roles and in a slightly revised form with a glazed nose for the bombardier training role. Production of the C.445M accounted for 404 of the eventual 1702 aircraft of the Goéland series. A number of aircraft were flown to the UK in June 1940 and operated wearing the Lorraine Cross of the Free French forces.

## SPECIFICATIONS

**COUNTRY OF ORIGIN:** France
**TYPE:** (C.445M) two-seat light transport with accommodation for six passengers
**POWERPLANT:** two 164kW (220hp) Renault 6Q-00/01 or -08/09 six-cylinder inverted inline engines
**PERFORMANCE:** maximum speed 300km/h (186mph); climb to 2000m (6560ft) in 10 minutes 15 seconds; service ceiling 5600m (16,570ft); range 1000km (621 miles)
**WEIGHTS:** empty 2300kg (5071lb); maximum take-off 3500kg (7716lb)
**WINGSPAN:** 17.60m (57ft 9in)
**LENGTH:** 13.80m (45ft 4in)
**HEIGHT:** 3.50m (11ft 6in)
**ARMAMENT:** none

# Consolidated B-24D Liberator

**P**roduced in a number of variants for a host of operational and training tasks, the Liberator was built in larger numbers (18,431 machines) than any other US warplane of World War II and was delivered in greater quantities than any other bomber in aviation history. First flown in December 1939, the single XB-24 prototype paved the way for seven YB-24 service test aircraft, then nine B-24A initial production machines with heavier defensive armament. The XB-24 was then upgraded to the XB-24B standard that led to the nine B-24C bombers, followed by the first major production models; the B-24D (2738 aircraft), generally similar B-24E (791 aircraft) and B-24G (430 aircraft with a power-operated nose turret). The B-24 made its operational debut in June 1942 with the long-range raids from Egypt against Hitler's Romanian oilfields. Pictured here is B-24D-85-CO *Teggie Ann*, the Group Lead Ship of the 47th Bomb Wing, 376th BG, painted in desert pink.

## SPECIFICATIONS

**COUNTRY OF ORIGIN:** United States
**TYPE** (B-24D) ten-seat long-range heavy bomber
**POWERPLANT:** four 895kW (1200hp) Pratt & Whitney R-1830-43 or -65 14-cylinder two-row radial engines
**PERFORMANCE:** maximum speed 488km/h (303mph); climb to 6095m (20,000ft) in 22 minutes; service ceiling 9755m (32,000ft); range 4586km (2850 miles)
**WEIGHTS:** empty 14,490kg (32,605lb); maximum take-off 27,216kg (60,000lb)
**WINGSPAN:** 33.53m (110ft)
**LENGTH:** 20.22m (66ft 4in)
**HEIGHT:** 4.46m (17ft 11in)
**ARMAMENT:** two 12.7mm (0.5in) trainable forward-firing machine guns in the nose, two 12.7mm (0.5in) trainable machines guns in each of the dorsal, ventral and tail turrets and one 12.7mm (0.5in) trainable lateral-firing machine gun in each of the waist positions, plus an internal bomb load of 3992kg (8800lb)

# Dornier Do 17Z

**D**evelopment of the Do 17E/F led to the Do 17M/P medium bomber/ reconnaissance types with Bramo 323 radial engines. These were followed by the Do 17S/U reconnaissance/pathfinder types that reverted to liquid-cooled engines but introduced a revised, shortened and enlarged forward fuselage of the glazed 'beetle eye' type. The 18 Do 17S/U pre-production types were followed by the definitive Do 17Z radial-engined model of which 522 were built. The three new-build variants were the Do 17Z-1 with a 500kg (1102lb) bomb load, Do 17Z-2 with an uprated powerplant and greater bomb load and Do 17Z-3 reconnaissance bomber, while conversions included the Do 17Z-4 dual-control trainer, Do 17Z-5 maritime reconnaissance, Do 17Z-6 long-range night-fighter with the distinctive nose of the Junkers Ju 88C-2 and Do 17Z-10 night-fighter with a redesigned nose. Pictured is a Do 17Z-2 of III/KG2.

## SPECIFICATIONS

**COUNTRY OF ORIGIN:** Germany
**TYPE:** (Do 17Z-2) four/five-seat medium bomber
**POWERPLANT:** two 746kW (1000hp) BMW Bramo 323P Fafnir nine-cylinder single-row radial engines
**PERFORMANCE:** maximum speed 410km/h (255mph); service ceiling 8200m (26,905ft); range 1500km (932 miles)
**WEIGHTS:** empty 5200kg (11,464lb); maximum take-off 8590kg (18,937lb)
**WINGSPAN:** 18m (59ft 1in)
**LENGTH:** 15.80m (51ft 10in)
**HEIGHT:** 4.60m (15ft 1in)
**ARMAMENT:** one or two 7.92mm (0.31in) trainable machine guns each in the windscreen, nose, dorsal and ventral positions, plus an internal bomb load of 1000kg (2205lb)

# Dornier Do 217

The Do 217 was Dornier's response to a 1937 requirement for a long-range warplane optimized for the heavy level and dive bombing roles. The Do 217 was essentially a scaled-up version of the Do 215 version of the Do 17 and first flew in August 1938. The first operational model was the Do 217E of which some 800 aircraft were built in Do 217E-0 to Do 217E-4 subvariants, with BMW 801 radial engines. These were followed by 950 examples of the Do 217K night bomber with a revised and unstepped nose and finally the Do 217M development of the Do 217K with DB 603 inverted-Vee engines. Prototype and pre-production variants were the Do 217C bomber, Do 217P high-altitude reconnaissance and Do 217R missile launching aircraft. There were also Do 217E and Do 217K subvariants armed with Hs 293 anti-ship missiles and Fritz-X guided bombs respectively. Do 217s sank the Italian ship *Roma* as she steamed to the Allies after Italy's surrender.

## SPECIFICATIONS

**COUNTRY OF ORIGIN:** Germany
**TYPE:** (Do 217E-2) four-seat heavy bomber
**POWERPLANT:** two 1178kW (1580hp) BMW 801ML 14-cylinder radial engines
**PERFORMANCE:** maximum speed 515km/h (320mph); initial climb rate 216m (740ft) per minute; ceiling 9000m (29,530ft); range 2800km (1740 miles)
**WEIGHTS:** empty 10,535kg (23,225lb); maximum take-off 16,465kg (36,299lb)
**WINGSPAN:** 19m (62ft 4in)
**LENGTH:** 18.20m (59ft 9in)
**HEIGHT:** 5.03m (16ft 6in)
**ARMAMENT:** one 15mm (0.59in) cannon in lower port side of nose, one 13mm (0.51in) machine gun in dorsal turret, one 13mm (0.51in) machine gun in ventral step position, 7.92mm (0.31in) forward-firing machine gun in nose, one 7.92mm (0.31in) machine gun in each cockpit side window; in the Do 217E-2/R19 subvariant, one remotely-controlled 7.92mm (0.31in) rearward-firing machine gun in the tail cone, plus a bomb load of 4000kg (8818lb)

# Douglas A-20

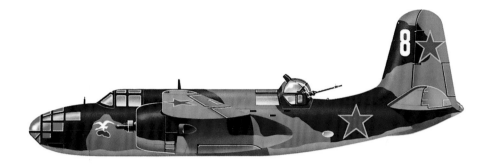

First ordered in June 1939, the A-20 was the American version of the light bomber initially bought by France and the UK as the DB-7 and Boston. The first US orders were for the A-20 and A-20A (63 and 143 aircraft) with supercharged and normally aspirated engines, the former being converted to P-70 night-fighters and the latter entering service in 1941. There followed 999 A-20Bs equivalent to the DB-7A, 948 A-20Cs with British equipment, 17 A-20E conversions from A-20A standard with the powerplant of the A-20B, 2850 A-20G attack bombers with a 'solid' nose and considerably heavier forward-firing armament, 412 A-20Hs with an uprated powerplant and 450 and 413 A-20Js and A-20Ks based on the A-20G and A-20H with a frameless transparent nose. The F-3 was a photo-reconnaissance conversion. Pictured here is a A-20B aircraft, fitted with a Russian dorsal turret, that served with the Black Sea Fleet Air Force in the spring of 1944.

## SPECIFICATIONS

**COUNTRY OF ORIGIN:** United States
**TYPE:** (A-20G) three-seat light attack bomber
**POWERPLANT:** two 1268kW (1700hp) Wright R-2600-23 14-cylinder two-row radial engines
**PERFORMANCE:** maximum speed 546km/h (339mph); climb to 3050m (10,000ft) in 8 minutes 48 seconds; ceiling 7225m (23,700ft); range 3380km (2100 miles)
**WEIGHTS:** empty 7708kg (16,993lb); normal take-off 10,964kg (24,127lb); maximum take-off 12,338kg (27,200lb)
**WINGSPAN:** 18.69m (61ft 4in)
**LENGTH:** 14.63m (48ft)
**HEIGHT:** 5.36m (17ft 7in)
**ARMAMENT:** six 12.7mm (0.5in) fixed forward-firing machine guns, two 12.7mm (0.5in) trainable machine guns in the dorsal turret and one 12.7mm (0.5in) rearward-firing machine gun in the ventral position; bomb load of 1814kg (4000lb)

# Douglas A-24

**W**hen it began to receive intelligence information about the Germans' successful employment of the Junkers Ju 87 dive-bomber in the early European campaigns, the US Army Air Corps decided to develop a similar capability. After evaluation of borrowed aircraft in 1940, the USAAC opted for the Douglas Dauntless already in service with the US Navy as the SBD. The first model ordered was the A-24 (eventually 178 aircraft) that was essentially similar to the SBD-3A; the first aircraft were delivered between July and October 1942. However, combat experience in the South-West Pacific theatre highlighted some fundamental deficiencies and later aircraft were used mainly for training. These later models were the A-24A and A-24B (170 and 615 aircraft) to SBD-4A and SBD-5 standards respectively. More than 40 A-24Bs were transferred to France in 1944. This aircraft wears the markings of the Free French Air Force.

## SPECIFICATIONS

**COUNTRY OF ORIGIN:** United States
**TYPE:** (A-24) two-seat dive-bomber
**POWERPLANT:** one 746kW (1000hp) Wright R-1820-52 nine-cylinder single-row radial engine
**PERFORMANCE:** maximum speed 402km/h (250mph); climb to 3050m (10,000ft) in 7 minutes; service ceiling 7925m (26,000ft); range 2092km (1300 miles )
**WEIGHTS:** empty 2804kg (6181lb); maximum take-off 4627kg (10,200lb)
**WINGSPAN:** 12.66m (41ft 7in)
**LENGTH:** 9.96m (32ft 8in)
**HEIGHT:** 4.14m (13ft 7in)
**ARMAMENT:** two 12.7mm (0.5in) fixed forward-firing machine guns in the upper part of the forward fuselage and two 7.62mm (0.3in) trainable rearward-firing machine guns in the rear of the cockpit, plus an external bomb load of 544kg (1200lb)

# Douglas A-26B Invader

Though only produced in small numbers by World War II standards, the A-26 has the distinction of having flown in more conflicts than any other warplane. The type was ordered in XA-26, XA-26A and XA-26B prototype forms; the first as a three-seat attack bomber a potential 2268kg (5000lb) bomb load, the second as a two-seat night-fighter and intruder with radar and cannon in a 'solid' nose and the third as a three-seat heavy attack fighter with a 75mm (2.95in) cannon in the 'solid' nose. The type first flew in July 1942 and the A-26B (1355 built) entered service in Europe during November 1944, at the same time, became operational in the Pacific. Powered by two 1491kw (2000hp) Pratt & Whitney radial engines that conferred a maximum speed of 571km/h (377mph), the A-26B was the fastest US bomber of the war.

Pictured here is A-26B-15-DT 'Stinky' of the 552nd Bomb Squadron, 386th

## SPECIFICATIONS

**COUNTRY OF ORIGIN:** United States
**TYPE:** (A-26B) three-seat light attack and reconnaissance bomber
**POWERPLANT:** two 1491kW (2000hp) Pratt & Whitney R-2800-27 or -71 18-cylinder two-row radial engines
**PERFORMANCE:** maximum speed 571km/h (355mph); climb to 3050m (10,000ft) in 7 minutes; service ceiling 6735m (22,100ft); range 2092km (1300 miles) with a 1361kg (3000lb) bomb load
**WEIGHTS:** empty 10,147kg (22,370lb); maximum take-off 12,893kg (42,300lb)
**WINGSPAN:** 21.34m (70ft)
**LENGTH:** 15.42m (50ft 7in)
**HEIGHT:** 5.64m (18ft 6in)
**ARMAMENT:** six 12.7mm (0.5in) fixed forward-firing machine guns, two 12.7mm (0.5in) trainable machine guns in dorsal barbette, two 12.7mm (0.5in) trainable rearward-firing machine guns in optional ventral barbette and provision for eight 12.7mm (0.5in) fixed forward-firing machine guns in four underwing packs, plus a bomb load of 2722kg (6000lb)

Bomb Group, US 9th Air Force, based at Beaumont-sur-Oise, France, in April 1945.

# Douglas A-26C Invader

The only other production model of the A-26 to see service during World War II was the A-26C, of which 1091 were delivered with a transparent nose for a bomb aimer's position and nose armament reduced to two guns. The type remained in service long after the war; the first conversion was for 150 JD-1 target-towing aircraft form A-26Cs for the US Navy. Some were later converted to launch and control missile test vehicles and drones, under the designation JD-1D. In 1948, USAF A-26B and A-26C aircraft were redesignated and became B-26B and B-26C respectively.

Both versions were heavily employed in the air war over Korea and, during the Vietnam War, some 70 aircraft were converted to B-26K standard for counter-insurgency operations. The RAF took possession of 140 Invader Mk 1s (A-26C) under the Lend-Lease scheme. Many other models were produced for a variety of roles, including photoreconnaissance and even executive transport.

## SPECIFICATIONS

**COUNTRY OF ORIGIN:** United States
**TYPE:** (A-26B) three-seat light attack and reconnaissance bomber
**POWERPLANT:** two 1491kW (2000hp) Pratt & Whitney R-2800-27 or -71 18-cylinder two-row radial engines
**PERFORMANCE:** maximum speed 571km/h (355mph); climb to 3050m (10,000ft) in 7 minutes; service ceiling 6735m (22,100ft); range 2092km (1300 miles) with a 1361kg (3000lb) bomb load
**WEIGHTS:** empty 10,147kg (22,370lb); maximum take-off 12,893kg (42,300lb)

**WINGSPAN:** 21.34m (70ft)
**LENGTH:** 15.42m (50ft 7in)
**HEIGHT:** 5.64m (18ft 6in)
**ARMAMENT:** two 12.7mm (0.5in) fixed forward-firing machine guns, two 12.7mm (0.5in) trainable machine guns in dorsal barbette, two 12.7mm (0.5in) trainable rearward-firing machine guns in optional ventral barbette and provision for eight 12.7mm (0.5in) fixed forward-firing machine guns in four underwing packs, plus a bomb load of 2722kg (6000lb)

# Douglas Boston Mk III

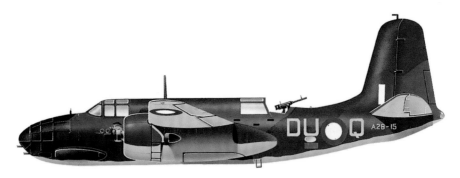

The DB-7 bombers taken over from French contracts (and powered by two R-1830-S3C4G radial engines with two-speed superchargers) were originally to have become Boston Mk II light bombers in British service, but, in the event, were adapted as Havoc Mk I night-fighters. The type entered service in April 1941 with No 85 Squadron. The next light bomber was thus the Boston Mk III, a designation applied to a total of 753 aircraft including 452 DB-7Bs taken over from France. The Boston Mk III had improved self-sealing fuel tanks, additional armour protection, a number of strengthening features to cater for a significantly increased maximum take-off weight, a slightly longer fuselage and increased fuel capacity. The aircraft were delivered to the UK from the summer of 1941 and entered service in October of the same year. Some aircraft were adapted as Boston Mk III (Intruder) machines with four 20mm (0.79in) cannon in a ventral pack.

## SPECIFICATIONS

**COUNTRY OF ORIGIN:** United States
**TYPE:** four-seat light attack bomber
**POWERPLANT:** two 1193kW (1600hp) Wright GR-2600-A5B Double Cyclone radial engines
**PERFORMANCE:** maximum speed 515km/h (320mph); initial climb rate 609m (2000ft) per minute; service ceiling 7470m (24,500ft); range 1996km (1240 miles) with reduced bomb load
**WEIGHTS:** empty 5534kg (12,200lb); normal take-off 8959kg (19,750lb); maximum take-off 9789kg (21,580lb)
**WINGSPAN:** 18.69m (61ft 4in)
**LENGTH:** 14.48m (47ft 6in)
**HEIGHT:** 5.36m (17ft 7in)
**ARMAMENT:** four 7.7mm (0.303in) fixed forward-firing machine guns on the sides of the forward fuselage, two 7.7.mm (0.303in) trainable machine guns in the dorsal position and one 7.7mm (0.303in) trainable machine gun in the ventral position, plus an internal bomb load of 907kg (2000lb)

# Douglas Boston Mk IIIA

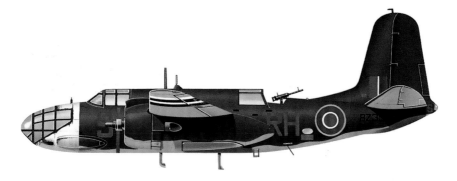

The Boston served in all theatres of the war and earned a well-deserved reputation for toughness and reliability. Pictured here is one of the many variants, the Boston Mk IIIA, in the colours of No 88 (Hong Kong) Squadron, Royal Air Force, at Hartford Bridge, Hampshire, on the eve of D-Day, June 1944. The aircraft wears USAAF olive-drab and grey camouflage with soluble white paint on the nose. The two under-fuselage smoke pipes were used to eject smokescreen trails to cover Allied movements during the Normandy landings. The Mk IIIA was the RAF designation for the Douglas A-20C Havoc, 140 of which were supplied to the RAF under the Lend-Lease scheme. This aircraft differed from the DB-7B previously mentioned in minor details, such as individual exhaust stacks to replace the collector rings. This helped to boost maximum speed by 24km/h (15 mph). A total of 958 A-20Cs were built, 808 by Douglas and 150 by Boeing.

## SPECIFICATIONS

**COUNTRY OF ORIGIN:** United States
**TYPE:** four-seat light attack bomber
**POWERPLANT:** two 1193kW (1600hp) Wright GR-2600-A5B Double Cyclone radial engines
**PERFORMANCE:** maximum speed 539km/h (335mph); initial climb rate 609m (2000ft) per minute; service ceiling 7470m (24,500ft); range 1996km (1240 miles) with reduced bomb load
**WEIGHTS:** empty 5534kg (12,200lb); normal take-off 8959kg (19,750lb); maximum take-off 9789kg (21,580lb)
**WINGSPAN:** 18.69m (61ft 4in)
**LENGTH:** 14.48m (47ft 6in)
**HEIGHT:** 5.36m (17ft 7in)
**ARMAMENT:** one 7.7mm (0.303in) fixed forward-firing machine guns on the sides of the forward fuselage, two 7.7mm (0.303in) trainable machine guns in the dorsal position and one 7.7mm (0.303in) trainable machine gun in the ventral position, plus an internal bomb load of 907kg (2000lb)

# Douglas C-47 Skytrain/Dakota

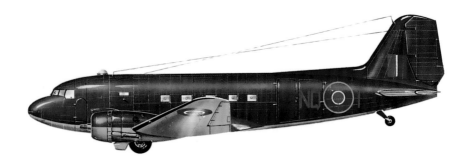

The DC-3 was developed from the DC-2 with greater power and accommodation increased to 21 and first flew in December 1935. Some 445 aircraft were built to civil orders, but the DC-3 remains better known in its military forms as the C-47 Skytrain, R4D and Dakota for the US Army Air Corps, US Navy and Royal Air Force respectively. Production of these and other military variants in the US totalled some 10,050 aircraft, excluding major production in Japan and the Soviet Union. These aircraft were truly war-winning weapons, providing the Western Allies with an unparalleled transport capability that expanded into paratroop and glider-towing capabilities as World War II progressed. Related developments were the C-48 to C-52 and C-68 impressments, plus the C-53 and C-117 personnel transports. Pictured here is a Douglas Dakota III of No. 24 Squadron, RAF. The squadron was actually a communications unit and flew Dakotas to Malta from 1943 onwards.

## SPECIFICATIONS

**COUNTRY OF ORIGIN:** United States
**TYPE:** (C-47) two/three-seat transport with accommodation for 28 troops, or 14 litters plus three attendants or 10,000lb (4536kg) of freight
**POWERPLANT:** two 895kW (1200hp) Pratt & Whitney R-1830-92 14-cylinder two-row radial engines
**PERFORMANCE:** maximum speed 370km/h (230mph); climb to 3050m (10,000ft) in 9 minutes 36 seconds; service ceiling 7315m (24,000ft); range 2575km (1600 miles)
**WEIGHTS:** empty 8103kg (17,865lb); maximum take-off 14,061kg (31,000lb)
**WINGSPAN:** 28.90m (95ft)
**LENGTH:** 19.63m (64ft 5.5in)
**HEIGHT:** 5.20m (16ft 11in)
**ARMAMENT:** none

# Douglas DB-7

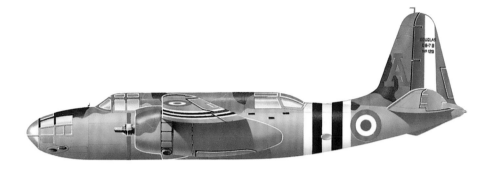

The Douglas DB-7 light attack bomber was a shoulder-wing monoplane of basically all-metal construction with a semi-monocoque fuselage, cantilever wing and retractable tricycle landing gear, and was initially bought by France. With the fall of Belgium and France by June 1940, however, the UK took over the outstanding orders for DB-7 warplanes intended for those countries. These were allocated the name Boston Mk 1. The first 20 machines to arrive were powered by two Pratt & Whitney R-1830-SC3G radial engines with single-speed superchargers. Four of them were in such poor condition that they were immediately struck off charge. The other 16 were ex-Belgian aircraft and, after a minimal modification programme (including a reversal of the throttle action to the British system of forward to open), were pressed into service as Boston Mk I conversion trainers. Pictured here is a DB-7B of GB I/19, French Vichy Air Force, Algeria, in autumn 1940.

## SPECIFICATIONS

**COUNTRY OF ORIGIN:** United States
**TYPE:** three-seat light attack bomber
**POWERPLANT:** two 820kW (1100hp) Pratt & Whitney R-1830-SC3G Twin Wasp 14-cylinder two-row radial engines
**PERFORMANCE:** maximum speed 475km/h (295mph); climb to 3660m (12,000ft) in 8 minutes; service ceiling 7835m (25,800ft)
**WEIGHTS:** empty 5171kg (11,400lb); maximum take-off 8636kg (19,040lb)
**WINGSPAN:** 18.67m (61ft 3in)
**LENGTH:** 14.32m (47ft)
**HEIGHT:** 4.83m (15ft 10in)
**ARMAMENT:** generally none, though provision was retained for 7.5mm (0.29in) fixed forward-firing machine guns on the sides of the forward fuselage, one 7.5mm (0.29in) trainable machine gun in the dorsal position and one 7.5mm (0.29in) trainable machine gun in the ventral position, plus an internal bomb load of 800kg (1764lb)

# Douglas DC-2

The DC-1 was the aeroplane that truly ushered in the era of the 'modern' cantilever low-wing monoplane transport with an all-metal structure, enclosed accommodation, retractable landing gear, nicely cowled engines and other features. It was designed to a requirement of Transcontinental and Western Air and first flew in July 1933, but was then developed as the more capable DC-2 that first took to the air in May 1934. The US forces were highly interested in the type but could not afford large-scale purchases, so, of the total production of 208 aircraft, only 64 were directly purchased by the US forces as the military C-32, C-33, C-34, C-39, C-41, C-42 and C-43 as well as the naval R2D. Of these, the variants procured in largest numbers were the C-33 and C-39 (18 and 35 machines). Some 24 civil DC-2s were also impressed for wartime service as C-32A aircraft. Pictured here is a KLM DC-2, based at Whitchurch in England throughout most of World War II.

## SPECIFICATIONS

**COUNTRY OF ORIGIN:** United States
**TYPE:** (R2D-1) two-seat transport with accommodation for 14 passengers
**POWERPLANT:** two 529.5kW (710hp) Wright R-1820-12 Cyclone nine-cylinder single-row radial engines
**PERFORMANCE:** maximum speed 338km/h (210mph); initial climb rate 305m (1000ft) per minute; service ceiling 6845m (22,450ft); range 1609km (1000 miles)
**WEIGHTS:** maximum take-off 8256kg (18,200lb)
**WINGSPAN:** 25.91m (85ft)
**LENGTH:** 18.82m (61ft 9in)
**HEIGHT:** 4.97m (16ft 4in)
**ARMAMENT:** none

# Douglas SBD Dauntless

The Dauntless was one of World War II's decisive warplanes, particularly in terms of its part in the Battle of Midway, despite it possessing only indifferent performance and poor manoeuvrability. As a result of these shortcomings, the type was phased out of first-line service well before the end of the war, despite only entering service in 1940. The first flight of the XBT-2 (converted Northrop BT-1) prototype was in April 1938. The main production models were the SBD-1 (57) with the 746kW (1000hp) R-1820-32 engine, SBD-2 (87) with heavier armament and more fuel, SBD-3 (584) with 12.7mm (0.5in) rather than 7.62mm (0.3in) machine guns, self-sealing fuel tankage and 24- rather than 12-volt electrics, SBD-4 (780) with detail improvements, SBD-5 (3025) with greater power and SBD-6 (451) with the 1007kW (1350hp) R-1820-66 engine. Shown is an SBD-5 Dauntless of Escuadron Aéreo de Pelea 200, Fuerza Aérea Mexicana.

## SPECIFICATIONS

**COUNTRY OF ORIGIN:** United States
**TYPE:** (SBD-5) two-seat carrierborne and land-based scout and dive bomber
**POWERPLANT:** one 895kW (1200hp) Wright R-1820-60 Cyclone nine-cylinder single-row radial engine
**PERFORMANCE:** maximum speed 410km/h (255mph); climb to 3050m (10,000ft) in 8 minutes; service ceiling 7780m (25,530ft); range 2519km (1565 miles)
**WEIGHTS:** empty 2905kg (6404lb); maximum take-off 4853kg (10,700lb)
**WINGSPAN:** 12.66m (41ft 7in)
**LENGTH:** 10.09m (33ft 1in)
**HEIGHT:** 4.14m (13ft 7in)
**ARMAMENT:** two 12.7mm (0.5in) fixed forward-firing machine guns in the upper part of the forward fuselage and two 7.62mm (0.3in) trainable rearward-firing machine guns in the rear of the cockpit, plus an external bomb load of 1021kg (2250lb)

# Fairey Albacore

The Albacore was designed to supersede the Fairey Swordfish as the primary torpedo bomber of the Fleet Air Arm. In fact, the Albacore was only able to complement the Swordfish in this role; the older aircraft outlived the Albacore by more than one year. Resulting from a 1936 requirement, the Albacore was in effect a modernized and technically somewhat improved development of the Swordfish with enclosed accommodation, a higher-rated engine, hydraulically operated flaps and a number of aerodynamic revisions designed to reduce drag. The first of two Albacore prototypes made its maiden flight in December 1938 and the first of 798 Albacore Mk I production aircraft entered service in March 1940, initially as a land-based type and, only from 1941, on board aircraft carriers. The Albacore spawned no improved models and was withdrawn from first-line service in 1944. Pictured here is an Albacore TB.Mk 1 of No 826 Squadron, Fleet Air Arm.

## SPECIFICATIONS

**COUNTRY OF ORIGIN:** United Kingdom
**TYPE:** (Albacore Mk I) three-seat carrierborne and land-based torpedo bomber and reconnaissance aeroplane
**POWERPLANT:** one 843kW (1130hp) Bristol Taurus XII 14-cylinder two-row radial engine
**PERFORMANCE:** maximum speed 257km/h (161mph); climb to 1830m (6000ft) in 8 minutes; service ceiling 6310m (20,700ft); range 1497km (930 miles)
**WEIGHTS:** empty 3269kg (7200lb); maximum take-off 5670kg (12,500lb)
**WINGSPAN:** 15.23m (50ft)
**LENGTH:** 12.18m (40ft)
**HEIGHT:** 3.81m (12ft 6in)
**ARMAMENT:** one 7.7mm (0.303in) fixed forward-firing machine gun in the leading edge of the starboard lower wing and one or two 7.7mm (0.303in) trainable rearward-firing machine guns in the rear cockpit, plus an external torpedo and bomb load of 907kg (2000lb)

# Fairey Battle

The Battle was an advance over the Hawker light bomber biplanes that it was designed to replace in Royal Air Force service. Nonetheless it was technically and tactically obsolescent by the time it entered service in March 1937, as a result of the rapid pace of aeronautical development during the approach to World War II. This is unsurprising, considering that the aeroplane was designed to meet a 1932 requirement, but did not fly until March 1936. Production of the Battle light bomber totalled 1818 from two British manufacturers for RAF service (subsequently redesignated as the Battle Mks I to V depending on the mark of engine installed) and 18 Belgian-built aircraft for Belgian service. The type was relegated to second-line service in 1940 as the Battle (T) trainer and Battle (TT) target-tug, of which 100 and 266 were built to supplement conversions. Shown here is one of the Battle trainer aircraft in September 1940.

## SPECIFICATIONS

**COUNTRY OF ORIGIN:** United Kingdom
**TYPE:** (Battle Mk II) two/three-seat light day bomber
**POWERPLANT:** one 768kW (1030hp) Rolls-Royce Merlin II 12-cylinder Vee engine
**PERFORMANCE:** maximum speed 406km/h (252mph); climb to 4570m (15,000ft) in 16 minutes 12 seconds; service ceiling 7925m (26,000ft); range 1931km (1200 miles) with a 644kg (1420lb) bomb load
**WEIGHTS:** empty 3361kg (7410lb); normal take-off 4944kg (10,900lb); maximum take-off 5307kg (11,700lb)
**WINGSPAN:** 16.45m (54ft)
**LENGTH:** 12.93m (42ft 5in)
**HEIGHT:** 4.57m (15ft)
**ARMAMENT:** one 7.7mm (0.303in) fixed forward-firing machine gun in the leading edge of the starboard wing and one 7.7mm (0.303in) trainable rearward-firing machine gun in the rear cockpit, plus an internal and external bomb load of 680kg (1500lb)

# Fairey Fox

**F**airey produced two types of Fox day bombers in the 1920s, namely the two-seat Fox Mk I with the Curtiss D-12 engine and the three-seat Fox Mk II with the Rolls-Royce Kestrel engine. Two-seat developments of the Fox Mk II, produced mainly by Fairey's Belgian subsidiary, served with the Belgian air force in the first part of World War II. The main variants were the Kestrel-engined Fox Mk II bomber mentioned previously, Fox Mk III reconnaissance fighter, Fox Mk IIIC with an enclosed cockpit and Fox Mk IIIS dual-control trainer. These were followed by the Hispano-Suiza-engined Fox Mk VI reconnaissance fighter, Fox Mk VII single-seat fighter and Fox Mk VIII improved version of the Mk VI. The type entered service in 1932, was wholly obsolete by the beginning of World War II and the 50 surviving aircraft suffered heavy losses at German hands. A seaborne reconnaissance version of similar design was the Fairey Seafox.

## SPECIFICATIONS

**COUNTRY OF ORIGIN:** Australia
**TYPE:** (Fox Mk VIR) two-seat reconnaissance fighter and light bomber
**POWERPLANT:** one 641kW (860hp) Hispano-Suiza 12-cylinder Vee engine
**PERFORMANCE:** maximum speed 365km/h (227mph); climb to 5000m (16,405ft) in 6 minutes 30 seconds; service ceiling 10,000m (32,810ft); range 600km (373 miles)
**WEIGHTS:** empty 1325kg (2920lb); normal take-off 2245kg (4950lb); maximum take-off 2345kg (5170lb)
**WINGSPAN:** 11.58m (38ft)
**LENGTH:** 9.17m (30ft 1in)
**HEIGHT:** 3.35m (11ft)
**ARMAMENT:** two 7.62mm (0.3in) fixed forward-firing machine guns in the upper part of the forward fuselage and one or two 7.62mm (0.3in) trainable rearward-firing machine guns in the rear of the cockpit, plus an external bomb load of 100kg (220lb)

# Fairey Swordfish Mk I

The Swordfish has an enduring reputation as one of the finest warplanes of World War II. This reputation resulted from its anachronistic biplane airframe and a combination of ruggedness, reliability, versatility in terms of weapons and equipment and such completely viceless handling characteristics that it could be flown in most weather conditions from aircraft carriers ranging in size from the largest fleet carriers to the smallest of escort carriers. The type, universally known as the 'Stringbag', resulted from a 1930 requirement for a carrierborne aeroplane to serve in spotter, reconnaissance and torpedo attack roles. The first of four prototype and pre-production aircraft flew in March 1933. Successful trials led to orders for an eventual 989 aircraft. Fairey built 689 and the remainder were Blackburn-built machines. Service deliveries began in July 1936 and, by the beginning of World War II, the FAA had 13 operational Swordfish squadrons.

## SPECIFICATIONS

**COUNTRY OF ORIGIN:** United Kingdom
**TYPE:** (Fairey Swordfish Mk I) two-seat torpedo-bomber
**POWERPLANT:**
**WEIGHTS:** empty 2359kg (5200lb); maximum take-off 4196kg (9250lb)
**WINGSPAN:** 13.87m (45ft 6in)
**LENGTH:** 11.07m (36ft 4in) with the tail up
**HEIGHT:** 4.11m (13ft 6in) with the tail up
**ARMAMENT:** one 7.7mm (0.303in) fixed forward-firing machine gun in the starboard side of the forward fuselage and one 7.7mm (0.303in) trainable rearward-firing machine in the rear cockpit, external bomb load of 1600lb (726kg)

# Farman F.221 and F.222

The F.220.01 bomber prototype was first flown in May 1932 and was then converted as a long-range mailplane. This was followed by the F.221.01 prototype that differed mainly in its redesigned vertical tail surface, fully enclosed nose and ventral gunner's positions, a semi-retractable 'dustbin' in place of the previous hatch position for the ventral gunner and a considerably uprated powerplant. Next were 10 F.221BN.5 bombers with enhanced defensive armament and then the F.222BN.5 that was produced in two variants as 11 F.222.1BN.5 machines with retractable main landing gear units and 24 F.222.2BN.5 machines with a lengthened nose and dihedralled outer wing panels. Some 29 aircraft were in service in 1939 and, before the fall of France, operated in the bomber role before being relegated to transport use up to 1944. Pictured here is an F.222.1 of the 2nd Escadrille, GB I/15, based at Reims-Courcy in May 1940.

## SPECIFICATIONS

**COUNTRY OF ORIGIN:** France
**TYPE:** (F.222.2BN.5) five-seat heavy night bomber
**POWERPLANT:** four 723kW (970hp) Gnome-Rhône 14N-11/15 radial engines
**PERFORMANCE:** maximum speed 320km/h (199mph); climb to 4000m (13,125ft) in 13 minutes 30 seconds; service ceiling 8000m (26,245ft); range 2000km (1243 miles) with a 2500kg (5511lb) bomb load
**WEIGHTS:** empty 10,500kg (23,148lb); normal take-off 15,200kg (33,510lb); maximum take-off 18,700kg (41,226lb)
**WINGSPAN:** 36m (118ft 1in)
**LENGTH:** 21.45m (70ft 5in)
**HEIGHT:** 5.19m (17ft)
**ARMAMENT:** one 7.5mm (0.29in) trainable forward-firing machine gun in the nose turret, one 7.5mm (0.29in) trainable machine gun in the dorsal turret and one 7.5mm (0.29in) trainable rearward-firing machine gun in the ventral 'dustbin' position, plus an internal bomb load of 4200kg (9259lb)

# Farman NC.223

The NC.223 (originally F.223) was a completely new aeroplane that retained a conceptual affinity to its F.222 predecessor. In overall terms, it was a blend of ancient and modern. In addition to the obsolete configuration retained from the F.222 bomber, the F.223 was also designed with the rectangular-section fuselage of the F.222. A revised tail unit with two vertical surfaces was added, but, in contrast to these drag-producing features, an excellent wing of modern stressed-skin concept with braced outer ends was used. The F.223.1.01 was a mailplane prototype, followed into the air during January 1938 by the NC.223.01 bomber prototype. This was followed by eight or possibly more NC.223.3BN.5 production aircraft that entered service during the Battle of France. The aircraft were then converted as transports. Shown here is Jules Verne, one of the NC.223.4 aircraft operated as long-range bombers by the French Air Force.

## SPECIFICATIONS

**COUNTRY OF ORIGIN:** France
**TYPE:** (NC.223.3BN.5) five-seat heavy night bomber
**POWERPLANT:** four 686kW (920hp) Hispano-Suiza 12Y-29 12-cylinder Vee engines
**PERFORMANCE:** maximum speed 400km/h (249mph); climb to 4000m (13,125ft) in 10 minutes; absolute ceiling 8000m (26,245ft); range 2400km (1491 miles)
**WEIGHTS:** empty 10,550kg (23,258lb); maximum take-off 19,200kg (42,329lb)
**WINGSPAN:** 33.58m (110ft 2in)
**LENGTH:** 22.00m (72ft 2in)
**HEIGHT:** 5.08m (16ft 8in)
**ARMAMENT:** one 20mm (0.79in) trainable cannon in the dorsal turret, one 20mm (0.79in) trainable rearward-firing cannon in the ventral turret and one 7.5mm (0.29in) trainable forward-firing machine gun in the nose position, plus an internal bomb load of 4200kg (9259lb)

# Fiat BR.20 Cicogna

The BR.20 Cicogna (stork) was the first 'modern' medium bomber produced in Italy leading up to World War II and first flew in prototype form in February 1936 for service from autumn of the same year. Delivery of 320 aircraft, including 85 for Japan and one for Venezuela, was followed by production of 264 improved BR.20M bombers. This model featured improved nose contours, revised armament and increased armour protection. The final variant was the BR.20bis (15 aircraft) with two 932kW (1250hp) Fiat A.82 RC.42S radial engines, a redesigned nose, two 7.7mm (0.303in) machine guns in waist positions and a power-operated dorsal turret. More than 160 Cicogna bombers were available when Italy entered World War II, with all but a handful lost before Italy's September 1943 armistice with the Allies. Pictured here is a BR.20M of the 4th Squdriglia, 11th Gruppo, 13th Stormo.

## SPECIFICATIONS

**COUNTRY OF ORIGIN:** Italy

**TYPE:** (BR.20M) five-seat medium bomber

**POWERPLANT:** two 768kW (1030hp) Fiat A.80 RC.41 14-cylinder two-row radial engines

**PERFORMANCE:** maximum speed 430km/h (267mph); climb to 5000m (16,405ft) in 17 minutes 56 seconds; service ceiling 7200m (23,620ft); range 1240km (770.5 miles) with a 1000kg (2205lb) bomb load

**WEIGHTS:** empty 6740kg (14,859lb); maximum take-off 10,340kg (22,795lb)

**WINGSPAN:** 21.56m (70ft 9in)

**LENGTH:** 16.17m (53ft 1in)

**HEIGHT:** 4.30m (14ft 1in)

**ARMAMENT:** one 7.7mm (0.303in) trainable forward-firing machine gun in the nose turret, two 7.7mm (0.303in) or one 12.7mm (0.5in) trainable rearward-firing machine guns in the dorsal turret and one 7.7mm (0.303in) trainable machine gun in the ventral hatch position, plus an internal bomb load of 1600kg (3527lb)

# Fieseler Fi 103 Reichenberg IV

This aircraft bears interesting comparison to the better known and more widely produced Fi 103, from which the V-1 flying bomb was developed. Long before that offensive commenced, the German high command were considering using piloted missiles to make precision attacks on high priority targets. With the war situation deteriorating, Hitler gave the go-ahead for such a project in March 1944 and the unmanned Fi 103 was adopted as the weapon best suited for use. By placing a cockpit and conventional flying controls in the body of the weapon, the designers were able to produce a controllable machine. The operational version was designated Fi 103R-IV and, although 175 were produced, none were ever used operationally. Flying this machine would have been an unenviable task for even the most skilled pilot. Once aimed at its target, he/she was expected to bale out.

## SPECIFICATIONS

**COUNTRY OF ORIGIN:** Germany
**TYPE:** piloted missile one 852kg (1874lb) warhead
**POWERPLANT:** one 350kg (772lb) thrust Argus 109-014 pulse jet
**PERFORMANCE:** maximum speed approximately 650km/h (404mph)
**WINGSPAN:** 5.72m (18ft 9in)
**LENGTH:** 8m (26ft 3in)
**ARMAMENT:** none

# Focke-Wulf Fw 200 Condor

The Condor is best remembered as the long-range reconnaissance aeroplane that searched for Allied convoys in the North Atlantic during World War II and then either attacked them directly with bombs/ missiles or vectored-in packs of German U-boats. However, the type was designed as a transatlantic airliner and first flew in this form during July 1937. The first of 259 Fw 200C military aircraft entered service in September 1939. A few of these aircraft were used as VIP transports, but the majority of the machines were long-range reconnaissance bombers in seven subvariants, some of which spawned their own subvariants with different armament fits, radar fits and provision for missile carriage and guidance, as well as stripped-down forms for special transport tasks. Pictured here is F8-BB, one of the first few 200C-1 Condors with a ventral gondola and full maritime and bombing equipment. It was assigned to Stab I/KG 40 and took part in the invasion of Norway.

## SPECIFICATIONS

**COUNTRY OF ORIGIN:** Germany
**TYPE:** (Fw 200C-3/U4) six-seat maritime reconnaissance bomber
**POWERPLANT:** four 895kW (1200hp) BMW-Bramo 323R-2 Fafnir nine-cylinder single-row radial engines
**PERFORMANCE:** maximum speed 360km/h (224mph); service ceiling 6000m (19,685ft); range 4440km (2759 miles)
**WEIGHTS:** empty 12,950kg (28,549lb); maximum take-off 22,700kg (50,044lb)
**WINGSPAN:** 32.84m (107ft 8in)
**LENGTH:** 23.46m (77ft)
**HEIGHT:** 6.30m (20ft 8in)
**ARMAMENT:** one 20mm (0.79in) trainable cannon in forward ventral gondola position, one 13mm (0.51in) trainable machine gun in rear dorsal position, one 13mm (0.51in) trainable machine gun in each beam position, one 7.92mm (0.31in) machine gun in rear ventral position and one 7.92mm (0.31in) machine gun in forward dorsal turret, plus a bomb load of 2100kg (4630lb)

# Fokker T.VIII-W

In 1936, the Dutch naval air service issued a requirement for a modern floatplane to replace the wholly obsolete Fokker T.IV-W floatplanes operated by itself and the air arm of the Netherlands East Indies Navy in the torpedo-bombing and reconnaissance roles. Fokker responded with the T.VIII-W design. This type was first delivered in 1939 and was produced in three forms. The first was the T.VIII-W/G of which 19 were delivered with a mixed metal and wood structure including a rear fuselage of wood. The second was the T.VIII-W/M of which 12 were delivered with a mixed structure including a light alloy rear fuselage and the third was the somewhat enlarged T.VIII-W/C of which five were delivered to Finland (one of them with wheeled landing gear) with two 663.5kW (890hp) Bristol Mercury XI radial engines. Pictured here is a Fokker T.VIII-Wg of Groep Vliegtuigen 4, Luchtvaartafdeling (Dutch Air Force) operating from Westeindermeer.

## SPECIFICATIONS

**COUNTRY OF ORIGIN:** Netherlands
**TYPE:** (T.VIII-W/G) three-seat maritime reconnaissance and torpedo bomber floatplane
**POWERPLANT:** two 335.5kW (450hp) Wright R-975-E3 Whirlwind nine-cylinder single-row radial engines
**PERFORMANCE:** maximum speed 285km/h (177mph); climb to 3000m (9845ft) in 7 minutes 48 seconds; ceiling 6800m (22,310ft); range 2750 km (1709 miles)
**WEIGHTS:** empty 3100kg (6834lb); maximum take-off 5000kg (11,023lb)
**WINGSPAN:** 18.00m (59ft)
**LENGTH:** 13.00m (42ft 8in)
**HEIGHT:** 5.00m (16ft 5in)
**ARMAMENT:** one 7.92mm (0.31in) fixed forward-firing machine gun in the port side of the forward fuselage, and one 7.92mm (0.31in) trainable rearward-firing machine gun in the rear of the cockpit, plus provision for an internal torpedo and bomb load of 600kg (1323lb)

# Gotha Go 244

The Go 242 was the German Air Force's standard transport glider in the second half of World War II. Deliveries totalled 1526 Go 242A and Go 242B gliders with skid and wheeled landing gear respectively. The success of the latter paved the way for the Go 244 that was, in essence, a powered version of the glider and evaluated with low-powered German or captured Soviet and French engines. The last were preferred and deliveries totalled 174 aircraft, including 133 Go 242B conversions. These were completed in forms corresponding to the five Go 242B production versions and were the Go 244B-1 freighter with torsion-bar shock absorption, Go 244B-2 freighter with wider-track main units and oleo shock absorption, Go 244B-3 and B-4 paratroop transport versions of the Go 244B-1 and B-2, plus the Go 244B-5 with dual controls and balanced rudders. Shown here is a Gotha Go 244B-1 of an unidentified Luftwaffe transport unit.

## SPECIFICATIONS

**COUNTRY OF ORIGIN:** Germany
**TYPE:** (Go 244B-2) two-seat transport with accommodation for 23 troops or freight
**POWERPLANT:** two 522kW (700hp) Gnome-Rhône 14M-4/5 14-cylinder two-row radial engines
**PERFORMANCE:** maximum speed 290km/h (180mph); climb to 5000m (16,405ft) in 18 minutes 30 seconds; ceiling 7650m (25,100ft); range 740km (460 miles)
**WEIGHTS:** empty 5225kg (11,517lb); maximum take-off 7800kg (17,196lb)
**WINGSPAN:** 24.50m (80ft 5in)
**LENGTH:** 15.80m (51ft 10in)
**HEIGHT:** 4.60m (15ft 1in)
**ARMAMENT:** one 7.92mm (0.31in) machine gun in cockpit roof position, one 7.92mm (0.31in) machine gun in tail of central nacelle, one 7.92mm (0.31in) machine gun in each side of central nacelle and provision for the troops to fire up to four 7.92mm (0.31in) machine guns from hold windows

# Grumman TBF Avenger

**M**aking a disastrous combat debut in the Battle of Midway (June 1942), the TBF rapidly became the classic torpedo bomber of World War II. The first of two XTBF-1 prototypes made the type's maiden flight in August 1941. Grumman then built only the TBF-1 model, whose total of 2289 aircraft completed by March 1945 included subvariants such as the baseline TBF-1, winterised TBF-1J Avenger, TBF-1P photo-reconnaissance type, TBF-1B (402 aircraft) delivered to the UK, TBF-1C (764 aircraft) with two 12.7mm (0.5in) machine guns in the wings, TBF-1CP photo-reconnaissance type, TBF-1D for the anti-submarine role with radar and underwing rockets, TBF-1E with air-to-surface radar and TBF-1L with a retractable searchlight for night illumination of submarines. The Royal Navy's wartime Avengers were mostly TBF-1Bs (404 received). In Fleet Air Arm service they were designated Tarpon Mk I and then Avenger Mk I in 1944.

## SPECIFICATIONS

**COUNTRY OF ORIGIN:** US

**TYPE:** (TBF-1C) three-seat carrierborne and land-based torpedo bomber

**POWERPLANT:** one 1268kW (1700hp) Wright R-2600-8 Cyclone 14 14-cylinder two-row radial engine

**PERFORMANCE:** maximum speed 414km/h (257mph); climb to 3050m (10,000ft) in 13 minutes; service ceiling 6525m (21,400ft); range 4321km (2685 miles)

**WEIGHTS:** empty 4788kg (10,555lb); maximum take-off 7876kg (17,364lb)

**WINGSPAN:** 16.51m (54ft 2in)

**LENGTH:** 12.42m (40ft 9in)

**HEIGHT:** 4.19m (13ft 9in)

**ARMAMENT:** two 12.7mm (0.5in) fixed forward-firing machine guns in the leading edges of the wing, one 12.7mm (0.5in) Browning trainable rearward-firing machine gun in the dorsal turret and one 7.62mm (0.3in) rearward-firing machine gun in ventral position, plus torpedo, bomb and rocket load of 1134kg (2500lb)

# Grumman TBM Avenger

With Avenger requirements far exceeding Grumman's production capabilities, the bulk of production was undertaken by the Eastern Aircraft Division of the General Motors Corporation, which produced the TBM model to the extent of 7546 aircraft up to September 1945. These were 550 TBM-1 and 2332 TBM-1C analogues of the TBF-1 and TBF-1C and then 4657 examples of the TBM-3 series with the more powerful R-2600-20 engine. The TBM-3 was produced in a number of subvariants similar to those of the TBM-1, but also including the TBM-3D with anti-submarine radar and the TBM-3E with podded anti-submarine radar. Many aircraft were transferred under Lend-Lease and numerous other subvariants appeared after the war for a number of increasingly important tasks. Pictured is one of the General Motors-built TBM-3 aircraft, operating from USS *Randolph*, part of Task Force 58 in January 1945.

## SPECIFICATIONS

**COUNTRY OF ORIGIN:** US

**TYPE:** (TBM-3E) three-seat carrierborne and land-based torpedo bomber

**POWERPLANT:** one 1417kW (1900hp) Wright R-2600-20 Cyclone 14 14-cylinder two-row radial engine

**PERFORMANCE:** maximum speed 444km/h (276mph); initial climb rate 628m (2060ft) per minute; service ceiling 9175m (30,100ft); range 3090km (1920 miles)

**WEIGHTS:** empty 4783kg (10,545lb); maximum take-off 8117kg (17,895lb)

**WINGSPAN:** 16.51m (54ft 2in)

**LENGTH:** 12.48m (41ft)

**HEIGHT:** 5.00m (16ft 5in)

**ARMAMENT:** two 12.7mm (0.5in) fixed forward-firing machine guns in leading edges of the wing, one 12.7mm (0.5in) Browning machine gun in dorsal turret and provision for one 7.62mm (0.3in) machine gun in ventral position, plus a torpedo bomb

# Handley Page Halifax

The Halifax was the main, but less glamorous partner to the Lancaster in the RAF heavy bomber force during the second half of World War II. It was a highly versatile warplane, undertaking maritime reconnaissance, transport and airborne forces roles. The two prototypes, the first of which flew in October 1939, were followed by the Halifax Mk I (84 aircraft in three series) that entered service in November 1940 with 954kW (1280hp) Rolls-Royce Merlin X Vee engines and the Halifax Mk II (1977 aircraft in three sub-series) with 1036kW (1390hp) Merlin XX or XXII engines. The Halifax Mk III saw a switch to Bristol Hercules radial engines; 2091 aircraft were made by five manufacturers. The Halifax Mk V, of which 904 were completed by two manufacturers in three sub-series, was an improved Mk II, delivered in both bomber and maritime reconnaissance forms. The aircraft shown has the markings of a Pathfinder unit.

## SPECIFICATIONS

**COUNTRY OF ORIGIN:** United Kingdom
**TYPE:** (Halifax Mk III) seven-seat heavy bomber
**POWERPLANT:** four 1204kW (1615hp) Bristol Hercules VI or XVI 14-cylinder two-row radial engines
**PERFORMANCE:** maximum speed 454km/h (282mph); climb to 6095m (20,000ft) in 37 minutes 30 seconds; service ceiling 7315m (24,000ft); range 3194km (1985 miles) with a 3175kg (7000lb) bomb load
**WEIGHTS:** empty 19,278kg (42,500lb); maximum take-off 29,484kg (65,000lb)
**WINGSPAN:** 30.07m (98ft 8in) or in later aircraft 31.59m (103ft 8in)
**LENGTH:** 21.74m (71ft 4in)
**HEIGHT:** 6.12m (20ft 1in)
**ARMAMENT:** one 7.7mm (0.303in) trainable forward-firing machine gun in the nose position, four 7.7mm (0.303in) trainable machine guns in the dorsal turret and four 7.7mm (0.303in) trainable machine guns in the tail turret, plus an internal bomb load of 6577kg (14,500lb)

# Handley Page Halifax B.Mk VI

First flown in October 1944 and built to the extent of 467 aircraft, the Halifax B.Mk VI was an improved Halifax Mk III intended for South-East Asian operations and therefore fitted with an uprated powerplant and an enlarged fuel capacity. A number of the aircraft were later converted as Halifax C.Mk VI 24-passenger transports as well as Halifax GR.Mk VI and Met.Mk VI maritime and meteorological reconnaissance machines. Another 193 aircraft were completed to Hercules B.Mk VII standard with 1204kW (1615hp) Hercules XVI engines and many of these machines were later converted as Halifax C.Mk VII 24-passenger transports. The Halifax A.Mk VII (234 aircraft) was a glider tug, some of which were also later converted as Halifax C.Mk VII 24-passenger transports, while the Halifax C.Mk VIII (96 aircraft) were 11-passenger transports. Further models were introduced following the end of World War II.

## SPECIFICATIONS

**COUNTRY OF ORIGIN:** United Kingdom
**TYPE:** (Halifax B.Mk VI) seven-seat heavy bomber
**POWERPLANT:** four 1249kW (1675hp) Bristol Hercules 100 14-cylinder two-row radial engines
**PERFORMANCE:** maximum speed 502km/h (312mph); climb to 6095m (20,000ft) in 50 minutes; service ceiling 6705m (22,000ft); range 1260 miles (2028km) with maximum bomb load
**WEIGHTS:** empty 17,690kg (39,000lb); maximum take-off 30,845kg (68,000lb)
**WINGSPAN:** 31.75m (104ft 2in)
**LENGTH:** 21.82m (71ft 7in)
**HEIGHT:** 6.32m (20ft 9in)
**ARMAMENT:** one 7.7mm (0.303in) trainable forward-firing machine gun in the nose position, four 7.7mm (0.303in) trainable machine guns in the dorsal turret and four 7.7mm (0.303in) trainable machine guns in the tail turret, plus an internal and external bomb load of 6577kg (14,500lb)

# Handley Page Halifax Mk III

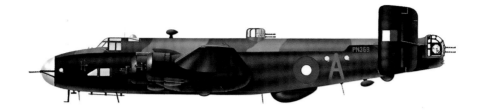

The slight superiority of the Lancaster over the Halifax in the night-bomber role meant that a number of comparatively early Halifax aircraft were made available for other roles. Halifax A.Mk III, for example, was the designation of Mk III bombers converted for the glider-towing role, while Halifax C.Mk III was the designation of Mk III bombers adapted as troop transports with fuselage accommodation for up to 24 men. The Halifax Mk III was also used for clandestine operations, two special duties squadrons (Nos 138 and 161) operating the type for the delivery of agents and equipment by parachute into German-held territory. No. 100 Group of Bomber Command operated Halifax bombers converted for the increasingly important electronic countermeasures role to degrade the capabilities of the Germans' radar and radio systems as an aid to other more conventional operations.

## SPECIFICATIONS

**COUNTRY OF ORIGIN:** United Kingdom
**TYPE:** (Halifax Mk III) seven-seat heavy bomber
**POWERPLANT:** four 1204kW (1615hp) Bristol Hercules VI or XVI 14-cylinder two-row radial engines
**PERFORMANCE:** maximum speed 454km/h (282mph); climb to 6095m (20,000ft) in 37 minutes 30 seconds; service ceiling 7315m (24,000ft); range 3194km (1985 miles) with a 3175kg (7000lb) bomb load
**WEIGHTS:** empty 19,278kg (42,500lb); maximum take-off 29,484kg (65,000lb)
**WINGSPAN:** 30.07m (98ft 8in) or in later aircraft 31.59 m (103ft 8in)
**LENGTH:** 21.74m (71ft 4in)
**HEIGHT:** 6.12m (20ft 1in)
**ARMAMENT:** one 7.7mm (0.303in) trainable forward-firing machine gun in the nose position, four 7.7mm (0.303in) trainable machine guns in the dorsal turret and four 7.7mm (0.303in) trainable machine guns in the tail turret, plus an internal bomb load of 6577kg (14,500lb)

# Handley Page Hampden

One of the most important medium bombers available to the British at the start of World War II, the Hampden was a good warplane, but was hampered by its narrow fuselage, which prevented crew members from taking over the task of another should he be injured. The Hampden prototype first flew in June 1937 and deliveries of the Hampden Mk I started in September 1938. Deliveries of this model amounted to 1430 aircraft from two British and one Canadian manufacturers, the last contributing 160 machines. Further capability came from the availability for training purposes of 100 Hereford aircraft that differed only in its powerplant of two 746kW (1000hp) Napier Dagger engines. Nine Herefords were converted to Hampden standard and, from 1942, some 141 surviving Hampden bombers were adapted as Hampden TB.Mk I torpedo-bombers for the anti-shipping role. Pictured is a TB.Mk 1 of an Operational Training Unit in 1942.

## SPECIFICATIONS

**COUNTRY OF ORIGIN:** United Kingdom
**TYPE:** (Hampden Mk I) four-seat medium bomber
**POWERPLANT:** two 746kW (1000hp) Bristol Pegasus XVIII nine-cylinder single-row radial engines
**PERFORMANCE:** maximum speed 426km/h (255mph); climb to 4570m (15,000ft) in 18 minutes 54 seconds; service ceiling 6920m (22,700ft ); range 3034km (1885 miles) with a 907kg (2000lb) bomb load
**WEIGHTS:** empty 5343kg (11,780lb); maximum take-off 10,206kg (22,500lb)
**WINGSPAN:** 21.08 m (69ft 2in)
**LENGTH:** 16.33m (53ft 7in)
**HEIGHT:** 4.55m (14ft 11in)
**ARMAMENT:** one 7.7mm (0.303in) fixed forward-firing machine gun in port side of the forward fuselage, one 7.7mm (0.303in) forward-firing machine gun in nose position, two 7.7mm (0.303in) machine guns in dorsal position, two 7.7mm (0.303in) machine guns in ventral position; bomb load of 1814kg (4000lb)

# Hawker Hart

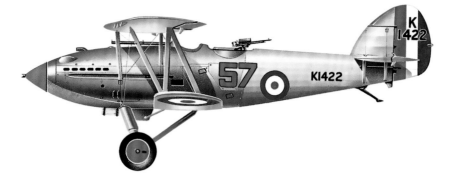

**A** classic warplane that emerged in the late 1920s and resulted in more aircraft of the basic and derived series than any other British aeroplane of the period between the two world wars, the Hart was the result of a 1926 requirement for a fast day bomber to replace the Airco (de Havilland) D.H.9A and Fairey Fawn. The design was based on the concept of maximum aerodynamic efficiency and the prototype made its maiden flight in June 1928. There followed 450 Hart Bomber, nine Hart Communications and 507 Hart Trainer aircraft for British service, as well as a number of export machines. These included ten dual control trainers that were built for the Royal Australian Air Force, which designated them Demon Mk II. The Hart was withdrawn from first-line service in the UK during 1938, but was still significant as a trainer after this time. A small number of the aircraft were operational in the Middle East and East Africa up to 1943.

## SPECIFICATIONS

**COUNTRY OF ORIGIN:** United Kingdom
**TYPE**: (Hart Bomber) two-seat light day bomber
**POWERPLANT**: one 391kW (525hp) Rolls-Royce Kestrel IB or XDR 12-cylinder Vee engine
**PERFORMANCE**: maximum speed 296km/h (184mph); climb to 3050m (10,000ft) in 8 minutes; service ceiling 6510m (21,350ft); range 756km (470 miles)
**WEIGHTS:** empty 1148kg (2530lb ); maximum take-off 2066kg (4554lb)
**WINGSPAN**: 11.35m (37ft 3in)
**LENGTH**: 8.94m (29ft 4in)
**HEIGHT**: 3.17m (10ft 5in)
**ARMAMENT**: one 7.7mm (0.303in) fixed forward-firing machine gun in the port side of the forward fuselage, and one 7.7mm (0.303in) trainable rearward-firing machine gun in the rear cockpit, plus an external bomb load of 263kg (580lb)

# Heinkel He 59

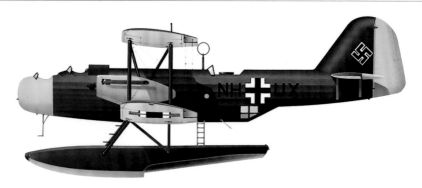

Designed in 1930, the He 59 resulted from a requirement for a torpedo bomber and reconnaissance warplane able to operate with equal facility on wheeled landing gear or twin-float alighting gear. The He 59b landplane prototype was the first to fly, an event that took place in September 1931, but it was the He 59a floatplane prototype that paved the way for the He 59B initial production model, of which 142 were delivered in three variants. Later developments were the He 59C-1 unarmed trainer, He 59C-2 air/sea rescue model, He 59D-1 combined trainer and ASR model, He 59E-1 torpedo-bomber trainer, He 59E-2 reconnaissance trainer and He 59N navigation trainer produced as He 59D-1 conversions. The trainer models survived slightly longer in service than the operational models, but all had been retired by 1944. Some aircraft were operated by Legion Condor in Spain in 1936. Pictured here is a Heinkel He 59 D-1 of the Luftwaffe in 1940.

## SPECIFICATIONS

**COUNTRY OF ORIGIN:** Germany

**TYPE:** (He 59B-2) four-seat coastal reconnaissance and torpedo-bomber floatplane with navigational training and air/sea rescue capabilities

**POWERPLANT:** two 492kW (660hp) BMW VI 6,0 ZU 12-cylinder Vee engines

**PERFORMANCE:** maximum speed 220km/h (137mph); climb to 2000m (6560ft) in 11 minutes 12 seconds; service ceiling 3500m (11,480ft); range 1530km (950 miles)

**WEIGHTS:** empty 5000kg (11,023lb); maximum take-off 9100kg (20,062lb)

**WINGSPAN:** 23.70m (77ft 9in)

**LENGTH:** 17.40m (57ft 1in)

**HEIGHT:** 7.10m (23ft 4in)

**ARMAMENT:** one 7.92mm (0.31in) trainable forward-firing machine gun in the nose position, one 7.92mm (0.31in) trainable rearward-firing machine gun in the dorsal position and one 7.92mm (0.3in) rearward-firing machine gun in the ventral position, plus torpedo and bomb load of 1000kg (2205lb)

# He 111H and He 111Z

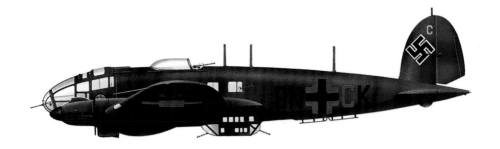

The definitive model of the He 111 series was the He 111H, which was in essence the He 111P with the revised powerplant of two Junkers Jumo 211 engines. The He 111H entered service in 1939 and production totalled about 6150 aircraft in major variants between the He 111H-1 and He 111H-23. These aircraft were characterised by a progressively uprated powerplant, increased fuel capacity, improved defensive as well as offensive armament, additional armour protection and provision for use in alternative roles such as anti-shipping attack, pathfinding, missile carrying and launching, paratroop delivery and glider towing. The introduction of the huge Messerschmitt Me 321 Gigant glider necessitated the development of the final variant, the He 111Z (Zwilling, or Twin), of which small numbers were produced as two He 111H-6 or -16 airframes joined by a new centre section carrying a fifth engine.

## SPECIFICATIONS

**COUNTRY OF ORIGIN:** Germany
**TYPE:** (He 111H-16) five-seat medium bomber
**POWERPLANT:** two 1007kW (1350hp) Junkers Jumo 211F-2 12-cylinder engines
**PERFORMANCE:** maximum speed 405km/h (252mph); climb to 4000m (13,125ft) in 23 minutes 30 seconds; service ceiling 8500m (27,890ft); range 1930km (1199 miles) with maximum bomb load
**WEIGHTS:** empty 8680kg (19,136lb); maximum take-off 14,000kg (30,865lb)
**WINGSPAN:** 22.60m (74ft 2in)
**LENGTH:** 16.40m (53ft 10in)
**HEIGHT:** 3.40m (13ft 2in)
**ARMAMENT:** one 7.92mm (0.31in) fixed machine gun in the nose, one 7.92mm (0.31in) machine gun in a nose position, one 7.92mm (0.31in) machine gun in dorsal position, one 7.92mm (0.31in) machine gun in rear of ventral gondola, two 7.92mm (0.31in) machine guns in each of two beam positions and one 7.92mm (0.31in) fixed machine gun in the tail cone, plus a bomb load of 2500kg (5511lb)

# Heinkel He 111P

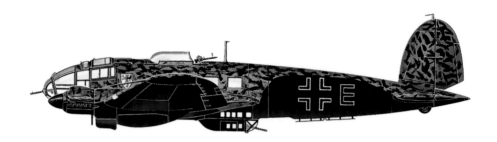

The Heinkel He 111 was Germany's most important medium bomber of World War II and, although ostensibly designed as a civil transport, had entered air force service by 1936 as the He 111B bomber with Daimler-Benz DB 601 engines and a conventional forward fuselage with a stepped cockpit. These 300 aircraft were followed by some 190 He 111E bombers with Junkers Jumo 211 engines and the next significant model, entering service in the spring of 1939, was the He 111P with the asymmetric fully glazed nose typical of all subsequent He 111 models. Built to the extent of some 400 aircraft in bomber and trainer subvariants between the He 111P-1 and He 111P-6, the He 111P was a useful type whose production was curtailed only by the reallocation of DB 601 engine supplies to fighters. Many He 111P-6 aircraft were later adapted as glider tugs. Spanish aircraft manufacturers built 236 He 111Hs under licence during and after the war as the CASA 2.111.

## SPECIFICATIONS

**COUNTRY OF ORIGIN:** Germany
**TYPE:** (He 111P-2) four-seat medium bomber
**POWERPLANT:** two 820kW (1100hp) Daimler-Benz DB 601A-1 12-cylinder engines
**PERFORMANCE:** maximum speed 398km/h (247mph); climb to 4500m (14,765ft) in 31 minutes 18 seconds; service ceiling 8000m (26,245ft); range 2400km (1491 miles
**WEIGHTS:** empty 8015kg (17,670lb); maximum take-off 13,500kg (29,762lb)
**WINGSPAN:** 22.60m (74ft 2in)
**LENGTH:** 16.40m (53ft 10in)
**HEIGHT:** 3.40m (13ft 2in)
**ARMAMENT:** one 7.92mm (0.31in) fixed machine gun in the nose, one 7.92mm (0.31in) machine gun in the nose position, one 7.92mm (0.31in) machine gun in dorsal position, one 7.92mm (0.31in) machine gun in rear of ventral gondola, two 7.92mm (0.31in) machine guns in two beam positions and provision for one 7.92mm (0.31in) fixed machine gun in the tail cone; bomb load of 2000kg (4409lb)

# Heinkel He 115A/B

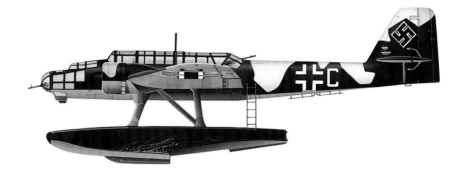

Resulting from a 1935 requirement for an advanced torpedo bomber floatplane that was also to be capable of undertaking a number of other coastal roles such as minelaying and reconnaissance, the He 115 V1 (first of four prototypes) made its maiden flight in August 1937. The He 115 was subsequently ordered into production early in 1938. Some 10 He 115A-0 pre-production aircraft were delivered from the summer of the same year and paved the way for 137 production machines. The first of these was the baseline He 115A (three subvariants including one for export), which was followed by the structurally strengthened He 115B. This in turn was operated in two main versions that spawned a number of minor subvariants for the torpedo, bombing, minelaying and reconnaissance roles. Many of these were built under licence by Weser Flugzeugbau. During the course of its career the aircraft served with Germany, Britain and Sweden.

## SPECIFICATIONS

**COUNTRY OF ORIGIN:** Germany

**TYPE:** (He 115B-1) three-seat coastal general-purpose and torpedo bomber floatplane

**POWERPLANT:** two 716kW (960hp) BMW 132K nine-cylinder single-row radial engines

**PERFORMANCE:** maximum speed 295km/h (183mph); service ceiling 5200m (17,600ft); range 2600km (1616 miles)

**WEIGHTS:** empty 6715kg (14,804lb); normal take-off 10,400kg (22,930lb)

**WINGSPAN:** 22.28m (73ft 1in)

**LENGTH:** 17.30m (56ft 9in)

**HEIGHT:** 6.59m (21ft 8in)

**ARMAMENT:** one 7.92mm (0.31in) trainable forward-firing machine gun in the nose position and one 7.92mm (0.31in) trainable rearward-firing machine gun in the dorsal position, plus an internal and external torpedo, bomb and mine load of 920kg (2028lb)

# Heinkel He 177A-1/3 Greif

The Greif (Griffin) was a potentially excellent but ultimately disastrous warplane on which Germany expended enormous and therefore largely wasted resources. The type was schemed as a bomber able to deliver a large bomb load over a considerable range at high speed and high altitude and, in an effort to extract maximum performance from a four-engined powerplant by the minimization of drag, it was decided that the pair of engines on each wing should be coupled to drive a single propeller. This coupled powerplant was beset by enormous technical problems that were never wholly cured and resulted in numerous inflight fires (the engines had a habit of catching fire without warning). The first of eight He 177 prototypes flew in December 1939 and slow development meant that it was the summer of 1942 before 130 He 177A-1 and 170 He 177A-3 early production aircraft entered service.

## SPECIFICATIONS

**COUNTRY OF ORIGIN:** Germany
**TYPE:** (He 177A-1/R1 Greif) five-crew heavy bomber
**POWERPLANT:** two 2013kW (2700hp) Daimler-Benz DB 606 (coupled DB 601) 24- cylinder engines
**PERFORMANCE:** maximum speed 510km/h (317mph); service ceiling 7000m (22,965ft); range 1200km (746 miles) with maximum bomb load
**WEIGHTS:** empty 18,040kg (39,771lb); maximum take-off 30,000kg (66,139lb)
**WINGSPAN:** 31.44m (103ft 2in)
**LENGTH:** 20.40m (66ft 11in)
**HEIGHT:** 6.39m (21ft)
**ARMAMENT:** one 7.92mm (0.31in) trainable forward-firing machine gun in nose position, one 20mm (0.79in) trainable forward-firing cannon in ventral gondola, two 7.92mm (0.31in) machine guns in ventral gondola, one 13mm machine gun in remotely controlled dorsal barbette, and one 13mm (0.51in) machine gun in tail position, plus a bomb load of 6000kg (13,228lb)

# Heinkel He 177A-5 Greif

In total, Heinkel and Arado together delivered 565 He 177A-5 aircraft and their operational record was much better than that of earlier versions. The most important Luftwaffe units to use the He 177 were KG 40 and KG 100, both taking part in revenge attacks against London during the early weeks of 1944. The A-6 version, of which six were built, had a pressurized cabin. However, the problems with the engines persisted. On February 1944, for example, 14 A-5s taxied out for a bombing raid on England. By the time the aircraft took off, one had already encountered mechanical problems and eight more soon returned to base with overheated or burning engines. Only four reached England to deliver their bomb loads and, of these, one was shot down. The aircraft pictured above is an A-5 of II Gruppe, which features a search radar and Hs 293A missiles under the wings for attacks against shipping.

## SPECIFICATIONS

**COUNTRY OF ORIGIN:** Germany

**TYPE:** (He 177A-5/R2) six-seat heavy bomber and anti-ship warplane

**POWERPLANT:** two 2311kW (3100hp) Daimler-Benz DB 610A/1/B-1 24-cylinder engines

**PERFORMANCE:** maximum speed 488km/h (303mph); climb to 6095m (20,000ft) in 39 minutes; service ceiling 8000m (26,245ft); range 5500km (3418 miles) with two Hs 293 missiles

**WEIGHTS:** empty 16,800kg (37,038lb); maximum take-off 31,000kg (68,343lb)

**WINGSPAN:** 31.44m (103ft 2in)

**LENGTH:** 22.00m (72ft 2in)

**HEIGHT:** 6.39m (21ft)

**ARMAMENT:** one 7.92mm (0.31in) trainable machine gun in nose position, one 20mm (0.79in) trainable cannon and two 7.92mm (0.31in) trainable machine guns in ventral gondola, two 13mm (0.51in) machine guns in remotely controlled dorsal barbettes, one 20mm (0.79in) cannon in tail; bomb load of 13,228lb (6000kg)

# Henschel Hs 123

Designed in 1934 and first flown in 1935 for service from 1936, the Hs 123 served in the Spanish Civil War and was technically obsolete by the time World War II started in 1939, but went on to play an important part in Germany's early successes and was still an important anti-partisan weapon in 1945. The Hs 123 was a sturdy single-bay biplane of fabric-covered metal construction with fixed tailwheel landing gear as well as an open cockpit and, although conceived as a dive-bomber, was generally operated in the close-support role. Here its great strength, considerable agility and stability as a gun platform offset its limited performance and comparatively light armament. Production of 604 Hs 123A-1 warplanes ended in 1938, but so useful was the type that there were calls in World War II for it to be returned to production. Pictured is an Hs 123A-1 of 7./Stukageschwader 165 'Immelmann' based at Fürstenfeldbruck in October 1937.

## SPECIFICATIONS

**COUNTRY OF ORIGIN:** Germany
**TYPE:** single-seat dive-bomber and close-support warplane
**POWERPLANT:** one 544kW (730hp) BMW 132A-3 nine-cylinder radial engine
**PERFORMANCE:** maximum speed 290km/h (180mph); climb to 2000m (6560ft) in 4 minutes 24 seconds; service ceiling 4100m (13,450ft); range 480km (298 miles) with a 200kg (441lb) bomb load
**WEIGHTS:** empty 1420kg (3131lb); maximum take-off 2350kg (5181lb)
**WINGSPAN:** 10.50m (34ft 5in)
**LENGTH:** 8.66m (28ft 5in)
**HEIGHT:** 3.76m (12ft 4in)
**ARMAMENT:** two 7.92mm (0.31in) fixed forward-firing machine guns in the upper part of the forward fuselage, plus an external bomb load of 450kg (992lb)

# Henschel Hs 129

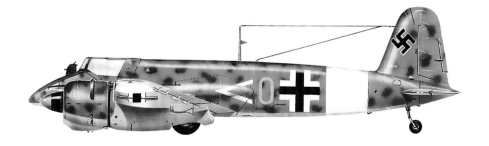

The Hs 129 was designed by Henschel in response to a spring 1937 requirement for a Schlachtflugzeug (battle aeroplane) that was to be relatively small, but heavily armoured for survivability as it provided close air support for the German ground forces. It emerged as a cantilever low-wing monoplane of all-metal construction and first flew in the spring of 1939 with two 347kW (465hp) Argus As 410 inverted-Vee engines. Development was slow as a result of the aeroplane's poor performance and handling in combination with the pilot's woeful fields of vision and it was only in April 1942 that the type entered service in its Hs 129B-1 form with an uprated powerplant of captured French radial engines. The aeroplane was still underpowered and the engines were both unreliable and very vulnerable to battle damage, but the demands of the campaign on the Eastern Front resulted in the delivery of 843 Hs 129B warplanes.

## SPECIFICATIONS

**COUNTRY OF ORIGIN:** Germany

**TYPE:** (Hs 129B-2) single-seat close-support and anti-tank warplane

**POWERPLANT:** two 522kW (700hp) Gnome-Rhône 14M-4/5 14-cylinder two-row radial engines

**PERFORMANCE:** maximum speed 407km/h (253mph); initial climb rate 486m (1595ft) per minute; service ceiling 9000m (29,530ft); range 560km (348 miles) with an underfuselage pack carrying one 30mm (1.18in) cannon

**WEIGHTS:** empty 4020kg (8862lb); maximum take-off 5250kg (11,574lb)

**WINGSPAN:** 14.20m (46ft 7in)

**LENGTH:** 9.75m (32ft)

**HEIGHT:** 3.25m (10ft 8in)

**ARMAMENT:** two 20mm (0.79in) fixed forward-firing cannon and two 13mm (0.51in) fixed forward-firing machine guns in the upper and lower sides of the fuselage, provision under the fusforward-firing cannon or four 7.92mm (0.31in) forward-firing machine guns; bomb load of 450kg (992lb)

# Ilyushin Il-2

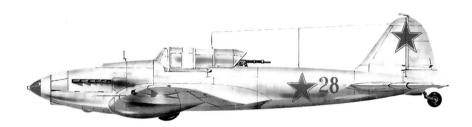

**B**uilt in larger numbers (36,150 aircraft) and at a higher rate than any other warplane in history, the Il-2 was instrumental in the Soviet defeat of Germany by 1945. The type entered service as the single-seat Il-2 three months before the German onslaught of June 1941. It was initially an indifferent warplane with the 1238kW (1660hp) AM-38 engine and an armament of two 20mm (0.79in) cannon and two 7.62mm (0.3in) machine guns, plus bombs and 82mm (3.23in) rockets. The aircraft matured into a formidable ground attack aircraft, much feared by German forces. The Il-2 was followed by the Il-2M with the AM-38F engine and 23mm (0.9in) cannon, the Il-2M Tip 3 two-seat version of the Il-2M to allow the provision of rearward defence and the Il-2M Tip 3M with 37mm (1.46in) rather than 23mm (0.9in) cannon for greater anti-tank capability. Shown here is an Il-2m3 in winter camouflage for the Stalingrad counter-offensive in 1943.

## SPECIFICATIONS

**COUNTRY OF ORIGIN:** Soviet Union
**TYPE:** (Il-2M Tip 3) two-seat close support and anti-tank warplane
**POWERPLANT:** one 1320kW (1770hp) Mikulin AM-38F 12-cylinder Vee engine
**PERFORMANCE:** maximum speed 415km/h (258mph); climb to 5000m (16,405ft) in 15 minutes; service ceiling 6000m (19,685ft); range 800km (497 miles)
**WEIGHTS:** empty 4525kg (9976lb); maximum take-off 6360kg (14,021lb)
**WINGSPAN:** 14.60m (47ft 11in)
**LENGTH:** 12m (39ft 5in)
**HEIGHT:** 3.40m (11ft 2in)
**ARMAMENT:** two 23mm (0.9in) fixed forward-firing cannon and two 7.62mm (0.3in) fixed forward-firing machine guns in the leading edges of the wings and one 12.7mm (0.5in) trainable rearward-firing machine gun in the rear cockpit, plus an internal and external bomb and rocket load of 1000kg (2205lb)

# Ilyushin Il-4

Designed as the DB-3f and first flown in January 1940 for service from 1941, the Il-4 was a modernized development of the DB-3M optimized for ease of production and field maintenance. The Il-4 remained in production up to 1944 and, with a total of 5256 aircraft, was among the Soviets' most important medium bombers of World War II. The first aircraft were powered by two 746kW (1000hp) Tumanskii M-88 radial engines, but these were soon replaced by uprated versions of the same engine. Other changes included during the production run included a four- rather than three-man crew, self-sealing fuel tanks and larger-calibre defensive weapons: the 7.62mm (0.3in) turret gun was replaced by a 12.7mm (0.5in) machine gun and then a 20mm (0.79in) cannon and the machine gun in the nose was changed to a 20mm (0.79in) cannon. Shown here is an Illyushin Il-4 (DB-3F) of a Red Air Force bomber regiment in 1944.

## SPECIFICATIONS

**COUNTRY OF ORIGIN:** Soviet Union
**TYPE:** four-seat long-range medium bomber
**POWERPLANT:** two 820kW (1100hp) Tumanskii M-88B 14-cylinder two-row radial engine
**PERFORMANCE:** maximum speed 420km/h (261mph); climb to 5000m (16,405ft) in 12 minutes; service ceiling 9400m (30,840ft); range 2600km (1616 miles) with a 1000kg (2205lb) bomb load
**WEIGHTS:** empty 5800kg (12,787lb); maximum take-off 10,300kg (22,707lb)
**WINGSPAN:** 21.44m (70ft 5in)
**LENGTH:** 14.80m (48ft 7in)
**HEIGHT:** 4.10m (13ft 6in)
**ARMAMENT:** one 7.62mm (0.3in) trainable forward-firing machine gun in nose position, one 7.62mm (0.3in) trainable machine gun in dorsal turret and one 7.62mm (0.3in) trainable rearward-firing machine gun in ventral hatch position, plus an internal bomb load of 2700kg (5952lb)

# Ilyushin Il-10

The Il-2 was a remarkably successful warplane, but its proven capabilities did not deter the Soviets from deciding in 1942 to press ahead with the creation of an improved ground-attack and anti-tank type. Various Ilyushin prototypes were evaluated before the decision came down in favour of the Il-10. This aircraft was clearly a linear descendant of the Il-2 but featured improved armour protection, a higher-rated engine, slightly smaller overall dimensions, considerably greater manoeuvrability and much enhanced performance. The Il-10 was ordered into production during August 1944, had fully replaced the Il-2 in production by November 1944 and entered service in February 1945. Some 3500 Il-10s were completed by the end of World War II, and the type remained in production and service until well after this time. The aircraft pictured bears the markings of a Polish air assault regiment in 1951.

## SPECIFICATIONS

**COUNTRY OF ORIGIN:** Soviet Union
**TYPE:** two-seat close support and anti-tank warplane
**POWERPLANT:** one 1491kW (2000hp) Mikulin AM-42 12-cylinder Vee engine
**PERFORMANCE:** maximum speed 551km/h (342mph); climb to 5000m (16,405ft) in 9 minutes 42 seconds; service ceiling 7250m (23,790ft); range 800km (497 miles)
**WEIGHTS:** empty 4680kg (10,317lb); maximum take-off 6535kg (14,407lb)
**WINGSPAN:** 3.5m (11ft 5.75in)
**LENGTH:** 13.40m (44ft)
**HEIGHT:** 11.10m (36ft 5in)
**ARMAMENT:** two 37mm (1.46in) fixed forward-firing cannon and two 7.62mm (0.3in) fixed forward-firing machine guns or four 23mm (0.9in) fixed forward-firing cannon in the leading edges of the wing and one 20mm (0.79in) trainable rearward-firing cannon in the dorsal turret, plus an internal and external bomb and rocket load of 1000kg (2205lb)

# Junkers Ju 52

The 18-seat Ju 52/3mg7e, shown here, was the major production variant featuring an automatic pilot and wide cabin doors to facilitate rapid loading and deployment of paratroopers. Subsequent versions had the wheel fairings removed, as they were found to clog with sand and mud. 'Auntie', as the Ju 52 was affectionately known to German troops, formed the backbone of the Luftwaffe transport fleet throughout World War II and served in every theatre with German forces. Pictured here is a Ju 52/3mg7e of 2.Staffel, KGrzbV 1, based at Milos in Greece, in May 1941 prior to the invasion of Crete. The operation, codenamed 'Mercury', involved para-dropping a sizable force from a fleet of 493 Ju 52s, but confusion over the drop zone and delays in providing support for the initial assault. Out of every four men who dropped on Crete, one was killed and, by the end of the operation, more than 170 Ju 52/3ms had been lost.

## SPECIFICATIONS

**COUNTRY OF ORIGIN:** Germany
**TYPE:** (Ju 52/3mg7e) three-seat transport with accommodation for 18 troops, or 12 litters, or freight
**POWERPLANT:** three 544kW (730hp) BMW 132T-2 nine-cylinder radial engines
**PERFORMANCE:** maximum speed 286km/h (178mph); climb to 3000m (9845ft) in 17 minutes 30 seconds; service ceiling 5900m (19,360ft); range 1305km (811 miles)
**WEIGHTS:** empty 6500kg (14,328lb); maximum take-off 11,030kg (24,317lb)
**WINGSPAN:** 29.20m (95ft 10in)
**LENGTH:** 18.90m (62ft)
**HEIGHT:** 4.52m (14ft 10in)
**ARMAMENT:** one 13mm (0.51in) or 7.92mm (0.31in) trainable rearward-firing machine gun in rear dorsal position, provision for one 7.92mm (0.31in) trainable machine gun in forward dorsal position and one 7.92mm (0.31in) trainable lateral-firing machine gun in each of the two beam positions

# Junkers Ju 52/3m

Intended as successor to the highly successful W 33 and W 34 transports, the Ju 52 was planned from the late 1920s as an enlarged version of the same basic design concept and first flew in prototype form during October 1930 with one 541kW (725hp) BMW VII Vee engine. The Ju 52a to Ju 52d initial production models for the civil market differed only in the type of engine used, but with the Ju 52/3m a three-engined powerplant was introduced for greater payload and performance. The series was built to the extent of some 4850 aircraft, the vast majority of them to meet military orders in variants between the Ju 52/3m ge and the Ju 52/3m g14e. The Ju 52/3m served initially as a bomber as well as transport, but in World War II was a transport and airborne forces aeroplane that saw operational use in every German theatre right up to May 1945. The aircraft pictured is a Ju 52/3mg6e equipped with a large magnetic loop for mine clearance operations.

## SPECIFICATIONS

**COUNTRY OF ORIGIN:** Germany
**TYPE:** (Ju 52/3m g7e) three-seat transport with accommodation for 18 troops, or 12 litters, or freight
**POWERPLANT:** three 544kW (730hp) BMW 132T-2 nine-cylinder radial engines
**PERFORMANCE:** maximum speed 286km/h (178mph); climb to 3000m (9845ft) in 17 minutes 30 seconds; service ceiling 5900m (19,360ft); range 1305km (811 miles)
**WEIGHTS:** empty 6500kg (14,328lb); maximum take-off 11,030kg (24,317lb)
**WINGSPAN:** 29.20m (95ft 10in)
**LENGTH:** 18.90m (62ft)
**HEIGHT:** 4.52m (14ft 10in)
**ARMAMENT:** one 13mm (0.51in) or 7.92mm (0.31in) trainable rearward-firing machine gun in rear dorsal position, provision for one 7.92mm (0.31in) trainable machine gun in forward dorsal position and one 7.92mm (0.31in) trainable lateral-firing machine gun in each of the two beam positions

# Junkers Ju 86

The Junkers Ju 86 was planned as a medium bomber. The first two production variants were the Ju 86D and Ju 86E that entered service in spring 1936 and differed in their powerplants, the latter type having 655kW (810hp) BMW 132 radial engines. Operational service revealed that performance was poor, so the type was then developed as the Ju 86B, Ju 86F and Ju 86Z civil transports, the Ju 86G bomber trainer and Ju 86K bomber for export. The final versions were the Ju 86P and Ju 86R for the high-altitude role with a pressurized cabin: the Ju 86P bomber had 708kW (950hp) Jumo 207A-1 engines and a span of 25.60m (84ft), while the Ju 86R reconnaissance type had 746kW (1000hp) Jumo 207B-3 engines and a span of 32m (105ft) for a ceiling of 14,400m (47,245ft). Production totalled 470 aircraft. Pictured is a Ju-86D-1 bomber of 5/Kampfgeschwader 254, based at Eschwege in September 1939.

## SPECIFICATIONS

**COUNTRY OF ORIGIN:** Germany
**TYPE**: two 447kW (600hp) Junkers Jumo 205C-4 vertically opposed diesel engines
**POWERPLANT:**
**PERFORMANCE:** maximum speed 325km/h (202mph); service ceiling 5900m (19,360ft); range 1140km (708 miles) with maximum bomb load
**WEIGHTS:** empty 5800kg (12,786lb); maximum take-off 8200kg (18,078lb)
**WINGSPAN:** 22.50m (73ft 10in)
**LENGTH**: 17.57m (58ft 7in)
**HEIGHT**: 5.06m (16ft 7in)
**ARMAMENT**: one 7.92mm (0.31in) trainable forward-firing machine gun in the nose position, one 7.92mm (0.31in) trainable rearward-firing machine gun in the dorsal position and one 7.92mm (0.31in) trainable rearward-firing machine gun in the retractable ventral 'dustbin', plus an internal bomb load of 1000kg (2205lb)

# Junkers Ju 87B-1

**W**ith its inverted-gull wing, massive landing gear and screaming dive trumpets, the Ju 87 remains synonymous with German success at the beginning of World War II. The Ju 87 was planned as a Stuka (short for *Sturzkampfluzeug*), or dive-bomber) a name that became synonymous with the type, to provide 'flying artillery' to support the armoured forces that would spearhead Germany's Blitzkrieg (lightning war) tactics. The Ju 87 first flew in 1935 with twin vertical tail surfaces and a British engine, but was then developed into the Ju 87A initial production model (200 aircraft) with a single vertical surface and the 507kW (680hp) Junkers Jumo 210 inverted-Vee engine. The Ju 87A entered service in the spring of 1937 and was soon supplanted by the Ju 87B-1 that was the first major model with a considerably uprated powerplant to provide improved performance, as well as allow a doubling of the bomb load.

## SPECIFICATIONS

**COUNTRY OF ORIGIN:** Germany
**TYPE:** two-seat dive-bomber and close support warplane
**POWERPLANT:** one 895kW (1200hp) Junkers Jumo 211Da 12-cylinder inverted-Vee engine
**PERFORMANCE:** maximum speed 383km/h (238mph); climb to 2000m (6560ft) in 4 minutes 18 seconds; service ceiling 8000m (26,245ft); range 790km (491 miles)
**WEIGHTS:** empty 2710kg (5974lb); maximum take-off 4340kg (9568lb)
**WINGSPAN:** 13.80m (45ft 3in)
**LENGTH:** 11.10m (36ft 5in)
**HEIGHT:** 4.01m (13ft 2in)
**ARMAMENT:** two 7.92mm (0.31in) fixed forward-firing machine guns in the leading edges of the wing and one 7.92mm (0.31in) trainable rearward-firing machine gun in the rear of the cockpit, plus an external bomb load of 500kg (1102lb)

# Junkers Ju 87B-2

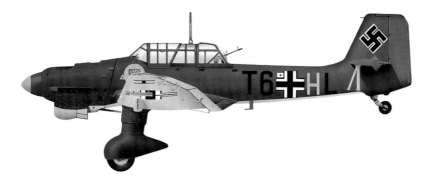

By the end of 1939, the Ju 87B-1 had been replaced in production by the Ju 87B-2 that introduced individual ejector exhaust stubs for a measure of thrust augmentation, hydraulically rather than manually operated radiator cooling gills, an improved propeller with broader-chord blades, and a bomb load of 1000kg (2205lb) when flown as a single-seater. Subvariants produced by the incorporation of factory conversion sets included the Ju 87B-2/U2 with improved radio, Ju 87B-2/U3 with extra armour protection for the close-support role and Ju 87B-2/U4 with ski landing gear. There was also a Ju 87B-2/Trop version for service in North Africa with sand filters and a pack of desert survival equipment and both this model and the Ju 87B-2 were delivered to Italy (which named them Picchiatello), while the Ju 87B-2 was delivered to Bulgaria, Hungary and Romania. At the beginning of World War II, Germany had 336 Ju-87B aircraft on strength.

## SPECIFICATIONS

**COUNTRY OF ORIGIN:** Germany
**TYPE:** two-seat dive-bomber and close support warplane
**POWERPLANT:** one 895kW (1200hp) Junkers Jumo 211Da 12-cylinder inverted-Vee engine
**PERFORMANCE:** maximum speed 383km/h (238mph); climb to 2000m (6560ft) in 4 minutes 18 seconds; service ceiling 8000m (26,245ft); range 790km (491 miles)
**WEIGHTS:** empty 2710kg (5974lb); maximum take-off 4340kg (9568lb)
**WINGSPAN:** 13.80m (45ft 3in)
**LENGTH:** 11.10m (36ft 5in)
**HEIGHT:** 4.01m (13ft 2in)
**ARMAMENT:** two 7.92mm (0.31in) fixed forward-firing machine guns in the leading edges of the wing and one 7.92mm (0.31in) trainable rearward-firing machine gun in the rear of the cockpit, plus an external bomb load of 1000kg (2205lb)

# Junkers Ju 87D

By the spring of 1940, the new Jumo 211J-1 inverted-Vee piston engine was ready for service and the Junkers design team set about evolving a development of the Ju 87B to exploit this engine, which offered not only greater power but also the possibility of a considerably cleaner installation. Other changes in the new variant were a complete redesign of the cockpit enclosure to reduce drag, a reduction in the size and complexity of the main landing gear fairings, an increase in the internal fuel capacity, improvement of crew protection through the introduction of more and thicker armour, the doubling of the defensive firepower and the strengthening of the lower fuselage and attached crutch for the ability to carry one 1800kg (3968lb) bomb. There were seven subvariants of the Ju 87D between the Ju 87D-1 and Ju 87D-8 for a variety of roles, ranging from glider-towing (Ju 87D-2) to night ground-attack (Ju 87D-7).

## SPECIFICATIONS

**COUNTRY OF ORIGIN:** Germany
**TYPE:** (Ju 87D-1) two-seat dive-bomber and close support warplane
**POWERPLANT:** one 1044kW (1400hp) Junkers Jumo 211J-1 12-cylinder inverted-Vee engine
**PERFORMANCE:** maximum speed 410km/h (255mph); climb to 5000m (16,405ft) in 19 minutes 48 seconds; service ceiling 7300m (23,950ft); range 1535km (954 miles)
**WEIGHTS:** empty 3900kg (8598lb); maximum take-off 6600kg (14,550lb)
**WINGSPAN:** 13.80m (45ft 3in)
**LENGTH:** 11.50m (37ft 9in)
**HEIGHT:** 3.88m (12ft 9in)
**ARMAMENT:** two 7.92mm (0.31in) fixed forward-firing machine guns in the leading edges of the wing and one 7.92mm (0.31in) trainable two-barrel rearward-firing machine gun in the rear of the cockpit, plus an external bomb load of 1800kg (3968lb)

# Junkers Ju 87G

As the increasing ineffectiveness of standard bombs against steadily more heavily armoured tanks became clear to the Luftwaffe in 1942, serious consideration was belatedly given to the adoption of more capable anti-tank armament for the Ju 87, which was now the service's primary anti-tank weapon. The obvious solution was a high-velocity cannon firing a moderately large projectile. The 37mm (1.46in) Flak 18 light anti-aircraft gun was selected and the revised weapon became the BK 37, which, with its magazine and long ejector chute for spent cases, was installed in a pod that could be positioned under the wing of the Ju 87 outboard of the main landing gear legs on hardpoints that could otherwise carry bombs. Validated on a Ju 87D-3 conversion, the new armament was introduced on the Ju 87G-1 that entered service in the autumn of 1942. This was the final operational version of the Stuka, with production of all versions totalling 5700.

## SPECIFICATIONS

**COUNTRY OF ORIGIN:** Germany
**TYPE:** two-seat anti-tank and close support warplane
**POWERPLANT:** one 1044kW (1400hp) Junkers Jumo 211J-1 12-cylinder inverted-Vee engine
**PERFORMANCE:** maximum speed 410km/h (255mph); climb to 5000m (16,405ft) in 19 minutes 48 seconds; service ceiling 7300m (23,950ft); range 1535km (954 miles)
**WEIGHTS:** empty 3900kg (8598lb)
**WINGSPAN:** 13.80m (45ft 3in)
**LENGTH:** 11.50m (37ft 9in)
**HEIGHT:** 3.88m (12ft 9in)
**ARMAMENT:** two 7.92mm (0.31in) fixed forward-firing machine guns in the leading edges of the wing, one 7.92mm (0.31in) trainable two-barrel machine gun in the rear of the cockpit and two 37mm (1.46in) fixed cannon under the wings, plus provision for an external bomb load as an alternative to the cannon

# Junkers Ju 87R

**P**roduced in parallel with the Ju 87B, the Ju 87R (Reichweite, or Range) was a long-range version of the Ju 87B for anti-ship and other long-endurance missions. The primary changes in the Ju 87R were a structural revision of the outer wing panels to incorporate two 150-litre (33imp gal) tanks that supplemented the standard pair of 240-litre (53 gal) tanks in the inboard wing panels and the introduction of 'plumbed' hardpoints under the outer wings, which thus carried two 300-litre (66 gal) drop tanks in place of the quartet of 50kg (110lb) bombs, so the bomb load was just one 250kg (551lb) weapon. The Ju 87R entered limited service in the spring of 1940, and was produced in four subvariants as the Ju 87R-1 to Ju 87R-4 – equivalent to the Ju 87B-1 to Ju 87B-4. During the Battle of Britain and in the latter stages of the war on the eastern front the Stuka proved vulnerable, particularly if no fighter cover was provided.

## SPECIFICATIONS

**COUNTRY OF ORIGIN:** Germany
**TYPE:** two-seat dive-bomber
**POWERPLANT:** one 895kW (1200hp) Junkers Jumo 211Da 12-cylinder inverted-Vee engine
**PERFORMANCE:** maximum speed 383km/h (238mph); climb to 2000m (6560ft) in 4 minutes 18 seconds; service ceiling 8000m (26,245ft)
**WEIGHTS:** empty 3187kg (7026lb)
**WINGSPAN:** 13.80m (45ft 3in)
**LENGTH:** 11.10m (36ft 5in)
**HEIGHT:** 4.01m (13ft 2in)
**ARMAMENT:** two 7.92mm (0.31in) fixed forward-firing machine guns in the leading edges of the wing and one 7.92mm (0.31in) trainable rearward-firing machine gun in the rear cockpit, plus an external bomb load of 500kg (1102lb)

# Junkers Ju 88A, D, H, S and T

R ivalling the Mosquito as the most versatile warplane of World War II and of vital importance to Germany right through this war, the Ju 88 was schemed as a high-speed level and dive-bomber and first flew in December 1936 for entry into service during 1939. The most important early model was the Ju 88A, of which some 7000 or more were delivered in variants up to the Ju 88A-17 with steadily uprated engines, enhanced defensive armament and improved offensive capability. Some 1450 of the Ju 88D, which was a long-range reconnaissance development, were delivered. The Ju 88H was another reconnaissance model of which small numbers were completed with 1267.5kW (1700hp) BMW 801 radial engines and the Ju 88S was a high-speed bomber of which modest numbers were produced with radial or Vee engines. The Ju 88T was a reconnaissance derivative of the Ju 88S. The final total of 15,000 Ju 88s of all models gives an idea of the significance of this aircraft.

## SPECIFICATIONS

**COUNTRY OF ORIGIN:** Germany
**TYPE:** (Ju 88A-4) four-seat high-speed, level and dive-bomber
**POWERPLANT:** two 999kW (1340hp) Junkers Jumo 211J-1/2 12-cylinder engines
**PERFORMANCE:** maximum speed 470km/h (292mph); climb to 5400m (17,715ft) in 23 minutes; service ceiling 26,900ft (8200m); range 2730km (1696 miles)
**WEIGHTS:** empty 9860kg (21,737lb); maximum take-off 14,000kg (30,865lb)
**WINGSPAN:** 20.00m (65ft 8in)
**LENGTH:** 14.40m (47ft 3in)
**HEIGHT:** 4.85m (15ft 11in)
**ARMAMENT:** one 7.92mm (0.31in) fixed or trainable forward-firing machine gun in windscreen, one 13mm (0.51in) or two 7.92mm (0.31in) forward-firing machine guns in nose position, two 7.92mm (0.31in) machine guns in rear of cockpit, and one 13mm (0.51in) or two 7.92mm (0.31in) trainable rearward-firing machine guns in rear of undernose gondola, plus a bomb load of 2500kg (5511lb)

# Junkers Ju 188

On the outbreak of World War II, the design of the Ju 288 as the Ju 88's successor was already well advanced, but by 1941, delays to the Ju 288 programme meant that an interim successor was required. The aircraft selected was the Ju 188, which had emerged from the Ju 88B prototype that had flown in 1940. The Ju 188 entered service in 1942 and production of about 1100 aircraft included the Ju 188A bomber with two 1324kW (1776hp) Junkers Jumo 213A engines, Ju 188D reconnaissance version of the Ju 188A, Ju 188E bomber with radial rather than Vee engines, Ju 188 reconnaissance version of the Ju 188E, Ju 188S high-altitude intruder and Ju 188T high-altitude reconnaissance aeroplane. Many other variants were trialled or projected for roles that included night-fighting and adverse-weather interception. Pictured here is one of the Ju 188D-2 aircraft on the strength of 1.(F)/124 based at Kirkenes in northern Finland during 1944.

## SPECIFICATIONS

**COUNTRY OF ORIGIN:** Germany
**TYPE:** (Ju 188E-1) four-seat medium bomber
**POWERPLANT:** two 1250kW (1677hp) BMW 801D-2 14-cylinder two-row radial engines
**PERFORMANCE:** maximum speed 544km/h (338mph); climb to 6000m (19,685ft) in 17 minutes 24 seconds; service ceiling 10,100m (33,135ft); range 2480km (1541 miles) with a 1500kg (3307lb) bomb load
**WEIGHTS:** empty 9410kg (20,745lb); maximum take-off 14,570kg (32,121lb)
**WINGSPAN:** 22.00m (72ft 2in)
**LENGTH:** 15.06m (49ft 5in)
**HEIGHT:** 4.46m (14ft 7in)
**ARMAMENT:** one 20mm (0.79in) trainable forward-firing cannon in nose position, one 13mm (0.51in) machine gun in dorsal turret, one 13mm (0.51in) rearward-firing machine gun in rear of cockpit and one 7.92mm (0.31in) two-barrel machine gun in undernose gondola, plus a bomb load of 3000kg (6614lb)

# Kawanishi H6K 'Mavis'

The H6K flying boat resulted from a 1933 requirement and was one of the best warplanes of the Imperial Japanese navy at the start of World War II's Pacific campaign. The type remained in useful service throughout the war as it was supplemented, although never really replaced, by the superb Kawanishi H8K 'Emily'. The first of four prototypes flew in July 1936 and successful trials led to the H6K2 production model, of which 10 were completed for service from January 1938 with four 746kW (1000hp) Mitsubishi Kinsei 43 radial engines. Further production comprised 127 examples of the H6K4 with revised armament and, in some aircraft, an uprated powerplant and 36 examples of the H6K5 with greater power. Lesser variants (with numbers) were the H6K2-L transport (16), H6K3 VIP transport (two) and H6K4-L transport (20), many of which remained in service until the end of the war. Pictured is an H6K5 of the Imperial Japanese Navy Air Force.

## SPECIFICATIONS

**COUNTRY OF ORIGIN:** Japan
**TYPE:** (H6K5) nine-seat maritime reconnaissance flying boat
**POWERPLANT:** four 969kW (1300hp) Mitsubishi Kinsei 51/53 14-cylinder two-row radial engines
**PERFORMANCE:** maximum speed 385km/h (239mph); climb to 5000m(16,405ft) in 13 minutes 23 seconds; service ceiling 9560m (31,365ft); range 6772 km (4208 miles)
**WEIGHTS:** empty 12,380kg (27,117lb); maximum take-off 23,000kg (50,706lb)
**WINGSPAN:** 40.00m (131ft 3in)
**LENGTH:** 25.63m (84ft 1in)
**HEIGHT:** 6.27m (20ft 7in)
**ARMAMENT:** one 20mm (0.79in) trainable rearward-firing cannon in tail turret, one 7.7mm (0.303in) machine gun in bow turret, one 7.7mm (0.303in) rearward-firing machine gun in dorsal position and two 7.7mm (0.303in) trainable lateral-firing machine gun in blister positions, plus a torpedo and bomb load of 3527lb (1600kg)

# Latécoére Laté 298

Designed to meet a 1933 requirement, the Laté 298.01 prototype first flew in May 1936. Successful trials led to the Laté 298 production model that entered service in the later part of 1938 with the French naval air arm, which received 24 and 12 (eventually 27) examples of the Laté 298A and Laté 298B with fixed and folding wings respectively. First ordered to the extent of five aircraft in April 1938, the Laté 298D was a Laté 298B development with a fixed wing and, in April and November, totals of 25 and 65 more aircraft were ordered. In the event, total deliveries amounted to only about 60 machines. In 1942, the Germans allowed a resumption of Laté 298 production against a Vichy French requirement for 30 aircraft, but it is uncertain how many of these Laté 298F machines (Laté 298D aircraft with simplified controls) were completed. Pictured here is a 298 of Escadrille T1, Aéronavale, based at Berre, near Marseilles, in late 1939.

## SPECIFICATIONS

**COUNTRY OF ORIGIN:** France
**TYPE:** (Laté 298D) three-seat coastal reconnaissance and torpedo-bomber floatplane
**POWERPLANT:** one 656kW (880hp) Hispano-Suiza 12Ycrs-1 12-cylinder Vee engine
**PERFORMANCE:** maximum speed 290km/h (180mph); climb to 1500m (4,920ft) in 5 minutes 39 seconds; service ceiling 6500m (21,325ft); range 2200km (1367 miles)
**WEIGHTS:** empty 3062kg (6750lb); maximum take-off 4800kg (10,582lb) in the reconnaissance role
**WINGSPAN:** 15.50m (50ft 10in)
**LENGTH:** 12.56m (41ft 3in)
**HEIGHT:** 5.23m (17ft 1in)
**ARMAMENT:** two 7.5mm (0.29in) fixed forward-firing machine guns in the leading edges of the wing, and one 7.5mm (0.29in) trainable machine gun in the rear of the cockpit, plus an external torpedo and bomb load of 670kg (1477lb)

# Lioré-et-Olivier LeO 451

The finest bomber developed by the French aero industry in the period leading up to World War II, the LeO 451 was an aesthetic masterpiece which helped to confirm in a very striking manner that French designers had finally abandoned the angular, slab-sided machines that had trundled about the skies of France throughout most of the 1930s. Resulting from a November 1934 requirement for an advanced four-seat day bomber, the first of two LeO 45.01 prototypes made its maiden flight in January 1937. These were followed by the LeO 451B.4 production model, which entered service in the autumn of 1939. Production was then rapid and deliveries totalled about 580 aircraft. The survivors continued in service after the fall of France, some being converted as 12-passenger civil and 17-passenger military transports, with a few remaining in service into the mid-1950s. The example shown here was on the strength of GB1/11 at Oran-La-Sénia (Morocco).

## SPECIFICATIONS

**COUNTRY OF ORIGIN:** France
**TYPE:** (LeO 451B.4) four-seat medium bomber
**POWERPLANT:** two 850kW (1140hp) Gnome-Rhône 14N-48/49 14-cylinder two-row radial engines
**PERFORMANCE:** maximum speed 495km/h (307mph); climb to 5000m (16,405ft) in 14 minutes; service ceiling 9000m (29,530ft); range 2300km (1429 miles) with a 500kg (1102lb) bomb load
**WEIGHTS:** empty 7815kg (17,229lb); normal take-off 11,400kg (25,133lb)
**WINGSPAN:** 22.52m (73ft 11in)
**LENGTH:** 17.17m (56ft 4in)
**HEIGHT:** 5.24m (17ft 2in)
**ARMAMENT:** one 7.5mm (0.29in) fixed forward-firing machine gun in the forward fuselage, one 20mm (0.79in) rearward-firing cannon in the dorsal turret and one 7.5mm (0.29in) machine gun in the ventral turret, plus an external bomb load of 2000kg (4409lb)

# LN (Loire-Nieuport) .40

First flown in LN.40.01 prototype form in June 1938, the LN.40 was schemed as a carrierborne dive-bomber for the French naval air arm. The first of 23 or more LN.401BP.1 production aircraft (out of an order for 42 machines) were delivered from mid-1939 for service with two shore-based units. The only other model to enter service was the LN.411BP.1, of which 40 were ordered by the French Air Force. The LN.411 was in essence a version of the LN.401 adapted for the solely land-based role by the removal of carrierborne features such as the arrester hook, wing-folding mechanism and flotation bags. Only a very small number was completed before the fall of France. Some 24 more LN.401 and LN.411 aircraft were completed in 1942 for the Vichy French air force through the assembly of existing components. The aircraft pictured here is an LN.401 that formed part of Escadrille AB.2 of the Aéronavale, based at Berck in France in May 1940.

## SPECIFICATIONS

**COUNTRY OF ORIGIN:** France
**TYPE:** (LN.401BP.1) single-seat carrierborne and land-based dive-bomber
**POWERPLANT:** one 514kW (690hp) Hispano-Suiza 12Xcrs 12-cylinder Vee engine
**PERFORMANCE:** maximum speed 380km/h (236mph); initial climb rate not available; service ceiling 9500m (31,170ft); range 1200km (746 miles)
**WEIGHTS:** empty 2135kg (4707lb); maximum take-off 2823kg (6224lb)
**WINGSPAN:** 14m (45ft 11in)
**LENGTH:** 9.75m (32ft)
**HEIGHT:** 3.50m (11ft 6in)
**ARMAMENT:** one 20mm (0.79in) fixed forward-firing cannon in an engine installation and two 7.5mm (0.29in) fixed forward-firing machine guns in the leading edges of the wing, plus an external bomb load of 225kg (496lb)

# Lockheed A-28 and A-29

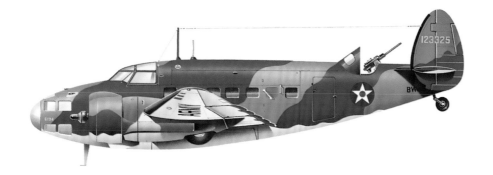

These designations were applied to versions of the Hudson built with US funding largely for deliveries under the Lend-Lease scheme to America's allies. The A-28 (52 with 783kW/1050hp Pratt & Whitney R-1830-45 engines) was delivered to Australia as the Hudson Mk IVA, while the A-28A (450 with a convertible trooping interior) was delivered to the UK as the Hudson Mk VI. The A-29 series had Wright R-1820 engines, and comprised the A-29 (416 with 895kW/1200hp R-1820-87 engines) that was delivered to the UK as 243 Hudson Mk IIIA aircraft with the others retained by the US, the A-29A convertible version of the A-29 (384) delivered to the UK as the Hudson Mk IIIA and the A-29B (24 conversions of the A-29 and A-29A for the photo-reconnaissance role) retained by the USA. There were also 217 and 83 AT-18 armed and AT-18A unarmed trainers. Pictured here is an A-29 of the US Army Air Corps, in pre-war markings and camouflage.

## SPECIFICATIONS
**COUNTRY OF ORIGIN:** United States
**TYPE:** (A-29) four-seat coastal reconnaissance bomber
**POWERPLANT:** two 895kW (1200hp) Wright R-1820-97 nine-cylinder single-row radial engines
**PERFORMANCE:** maximum speed 407km/h (253mph); climb to 3050m (10,000ft) in 6 minutes 18 seconds; service ceiling 8075m (26,500ft); range 2494km (1550 miles)
**WEIGHTS:** empty 5817kg (12,825lb); maximum take-off 9299kg (20,500lb)
**WINGSPAN:** 19.96m (65ft 6in)
**LENGTH:** 13.51m (44ft 4in)
**HEIGHT:** 3.63m (11ft 11in)
**ARMAMENT:** two 7.62mm (0.3in) fixed forward-firing machine guns in upper part of forward fuselage, two 7.62mm (0.3in) trainable machine guns in optional dorsal turret and one 7.62mm (0.3in) trainable rearward-firing machine gun in ventral position, plus an internal bomb load of 726kg (1600lb)

# Lockheed B-34 Lexington

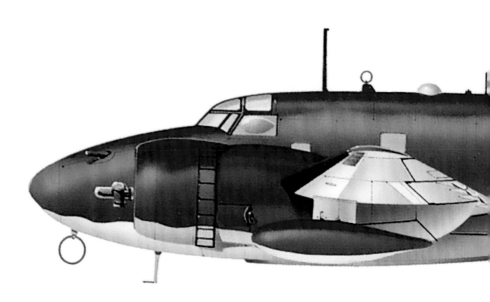

**B**-34 was the US Army Air Force designation for the 200 Ventura Mk IIA aircraft built with US funding for Lend-Lease delivery. The B-34A and B-34B were 101 and 13 aircraft repossessed from the production lines for service as 57 B-34A-2 bomber trainer, 28 B-34A-3 gunnery trainer, 16 B-34A-4 target tug and 13 navigator trainer aircraft. The B-37 (18 aircraft only built from an initial order for 550) was an armed reconnaissance derivative with two 1491kW (2000hp) R-2600-13 engines. The US Navy also operated a derivative of the Model 18 transport as the PV Ventura for the patrol bomber role. The core model was the PV-1, of which 1800 were built and 387 transferred to the UK as Ventura GR.Mk V machines. The US Marine Corps converted a few to use as nightfighters with British radar equipment and some PV-1 machines were converted as PV-1P photo-reconnaissance aircraft. The designation PV-3 was applied to 27 repossessed Ventura Mk II machines.

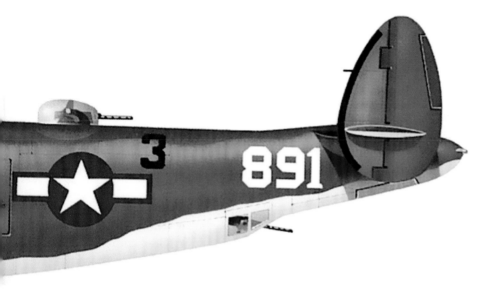

## SPECIFICATIONS

**COUNTRY OF ORIGIN:** United States

**TYPE:** (PV-1 Ventura) five-seat patrol bomber

**POWERPLANT:** two 1491kW (2000hp) Pratt & Whitney R-2800-31 Double Wasp 18- cylinder two-row radial engines

**PERFORMANCE:** maximum speed 518km/h (322mph); initial climb rate 680m (2230ft) per minute; service ceiling 8015m (26,300ft); range 2671km (1660 miles)

**WEIGHTS:** empty 9161kg (20,197lb); maximum take-off 15,422kg (34,000lb)

**WINGSPAN:** 19.96m (65ft 6in)

**LENGTH:** 15.77m (51ft 9in)

**HEIGHT:** 3.63m (11ft 11in)

**ARMAMENT:** two 12.7mm (0.5in) machine guns in upper part of forward fuselage; (late aircraft without bombardier's window had three 12.7mm/0.5in machine guns in an undernose gun pack), two 12.7mm (0.5in) machine guns in dorsal turret and two 7.7mm (0.303in) guns in ventral position; bomb load of 2268kg (5000lb)

# Lockheed Hudson

The Hudson was a development of the Model 14 Super Electra transport to meet a British and commonwealth coastal reconnaissance bomber requirement. It first flew in December 1938. The first of 351 Hudson Mk I aircraft reached the UK by sea in February 1939. Further deliveries of this important type included the Hudson Mk II (20 aircraft) with the same Wright R-1820-G102A engines but different propellers, Hudson Mks III and IIIA (about 428 and 601 aircraft) improved version of the Mk I with 895kW (1200hp) GR-1820-G205A engines, Hudson Mks IV and IVA (130 and 52 aircraft) with 918.5kW (1050hp) Pratt & Whitney R-1830-SC3G Twin Wasp engines, Hudson Mk V (409 aircraft) with 895kW (1200hp) R-1830-S3C4G engines and Hudson Mk VI (450 A-28A aircraft) delivered under Lend-Lease. Shown here is a Mk III of No 279 Squadron, RAF, based at Sturgate in 1942 and carrying an underfuselage load of an airborne lifeboat.

## SPECIFICATIONS

**COUNTRY OF ORIGIN:** United States
**TYPE:** (Hudson Mk I) six-seat coastal reconnaissance bomber
**POWERPLANT:** two 820kW (1100hp) Wright GR-1820-G102A Cyclone nine-cylinder single-row radial engines
**PERFORMANCE:** maximum speed 357km/h (222mph); climb to 3050m (10,000ft) in 10 minutes; service ceiling 6400m (21,000ft); range 3154km (1960 miles)
**WEIGHTS:** empty 5484kg (12,091lb); maximum take-off 8845kg (19,500lb)
**WINGSPAN:** 19.96m (65ft 6in)
**LENGTH:** 13.50m (44ft 4in)
**HEIGHT:** 3.32m (10ft 11in)
**ARMAMENT:** two 7.7mm (0.303in) fixed forward-firing machine guns in upper part of forward fuselage, two 7.7mm (0.303in) trainable machine guns in dorsal turret, two 7.7mm (0.303in) machine guns in beam positions and one 7.7mm (0.303in) machine gun in ventral position; internal bomb load of 612kg (1350lb)

# Lockheed Ventura

By mid-1939, Lockheed had the Hudson maritime reconnaissance bomber derivative of its Model 14 Super Electra civil transport in production for the UK. The company then started to consider further evolution along the same basic line, using the Model 18 Lodestar with its longer fuselage. Lockheed prepared a preliminary design and it was offered to the British in coastal reconnaissance and light bomber forms as successor to the Hudson and Bristol Blenheim respectively. The British approved of the light bomber idea, but the resulting Ventura Mk I (188 aircraft) that entered service in October 1942 was unsuccessful in the daylight bomber role and therefore retasked to the maritime role. Other orders included 487 Ventura Mk II (235 of them repossessed by the US), 200 Ventura Mk IIA, and 387 Ventura GR.Mk V machines. The Ventura served with all the Commonwealth nations, the Free French Air Force and also with the Brazilian Air Force.

## SPECIFICATIONS

**COUNTRY OF ORIGIN:** United States
**TYPE:** (Ventura GR.Mk V) five-seat coastal reconnaissance bomber
**POWERPLANT**: two 1491kW (2000hp) Pratt & Whitney R-2800-31 Double Wasp 18- cylinder two-row radial engines
**PERFORMANCE:** maximum speed 518km/h (322mph); initial climb rate 680m (2230ft) per minute; service ceiling 8015m (26,300ft); range 2671km (1660 miles)
**WEIGHTS:** empty 9161kg (20,197lb); maximum take-off 15,422kg (34,000lb)
**WINGSPAN:** 19.96m (65ft 6in)
**LENGTH:** 15.77m (51ft 9in)
**HEIGHT**: 3.63m (11ft 11in )
**ARMAMENT:** two 12.7mm (0.5in) machine guns in forward fuselage (late aircraft without bombardier's window had three 12.7mm (0.5in) machine guns in an undernose gun pack), two 12.7mm (0.5in) machine guns in dorsal turret and two 7.7mm (0.303in) machine guns in ventral position, plus a bomb load of 2268kg (5000lb)

# Martin B-10 and B-12

The first American-designed bomber to be flown in combat (albeit by an overseas air force), the B-10 bomber series was obsolete by the beginning of World War II, but in its time was a pioneering type. It was the first American bomber of all-metal construction to enter large-scale production, the first American warplane to be fitted with turreted armament and the US Army Air Corps' first cantilever low-wing monoplane. The USAAC received 151 examples of the B-10 and B-12 bombers, all retired before World War II, but some export aircraft saw combat service. The basic Model 139 was exported to Argentina, China, Thailand and Turkey (35, 9, 26 and 20 machines). The Japanese fought against the Chinese machines as well as the 120 Model 139W and Model 166 aircraft of the Netherlands East Indies in the late 1930s and early 1940s. Shown here is a Martin B-10B of the 28th Bombardment Squadron, US Army Air Corps, based at Luzon in the Phillipines from 1937 to 1941.

## SPECIFICATIONS

**COUNTRY OF ORIGIN:** United States
**TYPE:** (Model 139W) four-seat medium bomber
**POWERPLANT:** two 578kW (775hp) Wright R-1820 G-102 Cyclone 9-cylinder single-row radial engines
**PERFORMANCE:** maximum speed 322km/h (200mph); initial climb rate 567m (1860ft) per minute; service ceiling 7680m (25,200ft); range 950km (590 miles) with maximum bomb load
**WEIGHTS:** empty 4682kg (10,322lb); maximum take-off 7210kg (15,894lb)
**WINGSPAN:** 21.60 m (70ft 11in)
**LENGTH:** 13.46m (44ft 2in)
**HEIGHT:** 3.53m (11ft 7in)
**ARMAMENT:** one 7.62mm (0.3in) trainable forward-firing machine gun in nose turret, one 7.62mm (0.3in) trainable rearward-firing machine gun in dorsal position and one 7.62mm (0.3in) trainable rearward-firing machine gun in the ventral position, plus an internal and external bomb load of 1025kg (2260lb)

# Martin B-26 Marauder

The B-26 Marauder was one of the most important tactical warplanes operated by the US and its allies in World War II. The type was difficult for an inexperienced pilot to handle as a result of its high wing loading and high landing speed, but once mastered was an excellent warplane that achieved good results at a low loss rate. Entering service in summer 1941, the Marauder was built in a number of variants; the most important were the B-26 (201 machines), B-26A (139 machines with provision for a torpedo), B-26B and identical B-26C (1883 and 1235 machines with uprated engines and, in later aircraft, increased wing span), and B-26F and essentially similar B-26G (300 and 893 machines with increased wing incidence). The British designations for the B-26A, B, C and F/G were Marauder Mk I, IA, II and III respectively. The aircraft pictured is a B-26G-1 of the 456th Bomb Squadron, 323rd Bomb Group, US 9th Air Force, based at Laon-Athies in late 1944.

## SPECIFICATIONS

**COUNTRY OF ORIGIN:** United States
**TYPE:** (Marauder Mk I) seven-seat medium attack bomber
**POWERPLANT:** two 1379kW (1850hp) Pratt & Whitney R-2800-5 18-cylinder two-row radial engines
**PERFORMANCE:** maximum speed 507km/h (315mph) at 4570m (15,000ft); climb to 4570m (15,000ft) in 12 minutes 30 seconds; service ceiling 7620m (25,000ft); range 1609km (1000 miles)
**WEIGHTS:** empty 9696kg (21,375lb); maximum take-off 14,515kg (32,000lb)
**WINGSPAN:** 18.81m (65ft)
**LENGTH:** 17.07m (56ft)
**HEIGHT:** 6.05m (19ft 10in)
**ARMAMENT:** one 12.7mm (0.5in) trainable forward-firing machine gun in the nose position, two 12.7mm (0.5in) trainable machine guns in the dorsal turret and one 12.7mm (0.5in) trainable rearward-firing machine gun in the tail position, plus an internal and external bomb load of 4800lb (2177kg)

# Mitsubishi G3M 'Nell'

Although it was already obsolescent when Japan entered World War II in 1941, the G3M belied this technical limitation by scoring a number of stunning successes in the opening phases of Japan's offensive onslaught. The lack of an adequate replacement meant that the 'Nell' was forced to soldier on into total obsolescence and suffered devastatingly heavy losses. First flown in July 1935, the G3M was designed to provide the Imperial Japanese Navy Air Force with the means to project its air power deep into the Pacific. The variant that entered service in 1937 was the G3M1, but these 34 aircraft were soon supplanted by an eventual 993 examples of the G3M2 (uprated engines and greater fuel capacity) and G3M3 (further uprated engines and increased fuel capacity). Some aircraft were also converted as L3Y armed transport aircraft. Pictured here is a G3M3 of the Takao Kokutai, 21st Koku Sentai, operating from Hanoi during March 1941.

## SPECIFICATIONS

**COUNTRY OF ORIGIN:** Japan
**TYPE:** (G3M2) seven-seat medium attack bomber
**POWERPLANT:** two 801.5kW (1075hp) Mitsubishi Kinsei 41, 42 or 45 14-cylinder two-row radial engines
**PERFORMANCE:** maximum speed 373km/h (232mph); climb to 3000m (9845ft) in 8 minutes 19 seconds; service ceiling 9130m (29,950ft); range 4380km (2722 miles)
**WEIGHTS:** empty 4965kg (10,936lb); maximum take-off 8000kg (17,637lb)
**WINGSPAN:** 25m (82ft)
**LENGTH:** 16.45m (54ft)
**HEIGHT:** 3.69m (12ft 1in)
**ARMAMENT:** one 20mm (0.79in) trainable rearward-firing cannon in dorsal turret, one 7.7mm (0.303in) trainable machine gun in retractable dorsal turret, one 7.7mm (0.303in) machine gun in each beam position and provision for one 7.7mm (0.303in) machine gun in cockpit, plus a bomb load of 800kg (1764lb)

# Mitsubishi G4M1 'Betty'

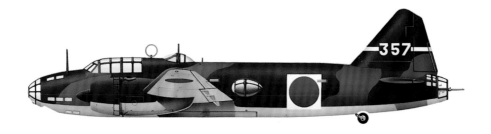

The G4M was the ultimate expression of the Imperial Japanese Navy Air Force's desire to project land-based air power from its island garrisons deep into the Pacific Ocean for the destruction of enemy warships and the support of its own forces' amphibious operations. The G4M certainly possessed remarkable range but, as combat was to prove, this capability was purchased only at the expense of features that were just as important: crew protection, self-sealing fuel tanks and a sturdy structure able to absorb battle damage. Resulting from a 1937 requirement, the first of two G4M1 prototypes flew in October 1939, and the type entered service early in 1941. Production totalled 1200 G4M1 aircraft in variants such as the Convoy Fighter escort (five 20mm/0.79in trainable cannon), Model 11 attack bomber and Model 12 attack bomber, the last with MK4E engines. Trainer and transport variants were then created as conversions. Pictured is a G4M1 of the 708th Kokutai.

## SPECIFICATIONS

**COUNTRY OF ORIGIN:** Japan
**TYPE:** (G4M1 Model 11) seven-seat medium attack bomber
**POWERPLANT:** two 1141kW (1530hp) Mitsubishi MK4A Kasei 11 14-cylinder two-row radial engines
**PERFORMANCE:** maximum speed 428km/h (266mph); climb to 7000m (22,965ft) in 18 minutes; range 6033km (3749 miles)
**WEIGHTS:** empty 6800kg (14,991lb); maximum take-off 9500kg (20,944lb)
**WINGSPAN:** 25.00m (82ft)
**LENGTH:** 20.00m (65ft 7in)
**HEIGHT:** 6.00m (19ft 8in)
**ARMAMENT:** one 20mm (0.79in) trainable rearward-firing cannon in the tail position, one 7.7mm (0.303in) trainable rearward-firing machine gun in the dorsal blister position and one 7.7mm (0.303in) trainable lateral-firing machine gun in each of the two beam positions, plus an external bomb and torpedo load of 800kg (1764lb)

# Mitsubishi G4M2 'Betty'

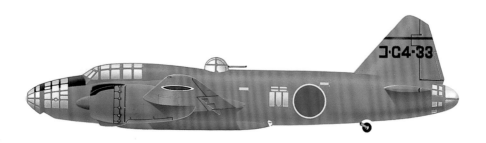

Following the G4M1, the G4M2 was built to the extent of 1154 aircraft for service from mid-1943 with an uprated powerplant, a laminar-flow wing, a larger tailplane, additional fuel capacity and heavier defensive armament for better overall capability, but only at the cost of reduced agility. There were three attack bomber Model 22 subvariants (about 350 aircraft) with different armaments and four attack bomber Model 24 subvariants (about 790 aircraft) with 1379kW (1850hp) MK4T engines and different armaments. A small number of aircraft were converted as engine test beds and some machines were adapted as Model 24J carriers for the Yokosuka MXY7 Okha rocket-powered *kamikaze* warplane. The G4M2 remained in service right to the end of World War II. The delegation bringing the final declaration of surrender from the Japanese high command was brought to Ie-Shima in two 'Bettys'.

## SPECIFICATIONS

**COUNTRY OF ORIGIN:** Japan
**TYPE:** (G4M2 Model 22) seven-seat medium attack bomber
**POWERPLANT:** two 1342kW (1800hp) Mitsubishi MK4P Kasei 21 14-cylinder two-row radial engines
**PERFORMANCE:** maximum speed 438km/h (272mph); climb to 8000m (26,245ft) in 30 minutes 24 seconds; range 6059km (3765 miles)
**WEIGHTS:** empty 8160kg (17,990lb); maximum take-off 12,500kg (27,557lb)
**WINGSPAN:** 25.00m (82ft)
**LENGTH:** 20.00m (65ft 7in)
**HEIGHT:** 6.00m (19ft 8in)
**ARMAMENT:** two 7.7mm (0.303in) trainable forward-firing machine guns in nose position, one 20mm (0.79in) trainable cannon in dorsal turret, one 20mm (0.79in) trainable lateral-firing cannon in each beam position and one 20mm (0.79in) trainable rearward-firing cannon in tail position, plus a bomb and torpedo load of 800kg (1764lb)

# Mitsubishi G4M3 'Betty'

**B**y the second half of 1942, the Imperial Japanese Navy Air Force had belatedly realised that the G4M had a major problem of survivability as a result of its lack of armour protection and self-sealing fuel tanks. Many crew members and aircraft were lost as a result after they had been hit and caught fire. In November 1942, therefore, Mitsubishi began work on the G4M3 with armour for the crew areas and the wing revised with self-sealing tanks. At the same time the opportunity was taken to improve the tail gunner's position along the lines of American aircraft, the consequent shortening of the fuselage and forward movement of the centre of gravity requiring the introduction of dihedral on the tailplane to restore stability. However, the G4M3 entered too late to be of any real use and only 60 of these Attack Bomber Model 34 aircraft had been completed before Japan's surrender in August 1945.

## SPECIFICATIONS

**COUNTRY OF ORIGIN:** Japan
**TYPE:** (G4M3) seven-seat medium attack bomber
**POWERPLANT:** two 1361kW (1825hp) Mitsubishi MK4T Kasei 25 14-cylinder two-row radial engines
**PERFORMANCE:** maximum speed 470km/h (292mph); climb to 7000m (22,965ft) in 20 minutes 10 seconds; service ceiling 9200m (30,185ft); range 4335km (2694 miles)
**WEIGHTS:** empty 8350kg (18,409lb); maximum take-off 12,500kg (27,558lb)
**WINGSPAN:** 25m (82ft)
**LENGTH:** 19.50m (64ft)
**HEIGHT:** 6m (19ft 8in)
**ARMAMENT:** two 7.7mm (0.303in) trainable forward-firing machine guns in nose, one 20mm (0.79in) trainable cannon in dorsal turret, one 20mm (0.79in) trainable cannon in each beam position and one 20mm (0.79in) trainable rearward-firing cannon in tail position, plus a bomb load of 800kg (1764lb)

# Mitsubishi Ki-21 'Sally' and 'Gwen'

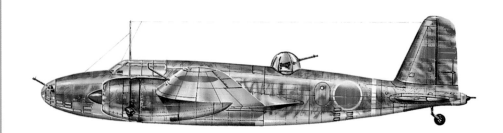

The best bomber that was available in significant numbers to the Imperial Japanese Army Air Force in World War II, the Ki-21 was yet another example of Japan's short-sighted policy of insisting on high speed and long range, achieved only by sacrificing protection, defensive firepower and offensive warload. The type resulted from a February 1936 requirement for a modern bomber and the first of eight prototypes made its maiden flight in December 1936. The Ki-21 entered service in mid-1938; production totalled 774 examples of the Ki-21-I with 634kW (850hp) Nakajima Ha-5 radial engines in three subvariants differentiated by their defensive armaments and fuel capacities, and 1278 examples of the Ki-21-II with a different and uprated powerplant in two subvariants. Some Ki-21-Is were converted as MC-21 unarmed civil transports. Pictured here is a Ki-21-IIb of the Imperial Japanese Army Air Service in 1944.

## SPECIFICATIONS

**COUNTRY OF ORIGIN:** Japan
**TYPE:** (Ki-21-IIb) five/seven-seat 'heavy' (actually medium) bomber
**POWERPLANT:** two 1118kW (1500hp) Mitsubishi Ha-101 (Army Type: 100) 14-cylinder two-row radial engines
**PERFORMANCE:** maximum speed 486km/h (302mph); climb to 6000m (19,685ft) in 13 minutes 13 seconds; service ceiling 10,000m (32,810ft); range 2700km (1678 miles)
**WEIGHTS:** empty 6070kg (13,382lb); maximum take-off 10,610kg (23,391lb)
**WINGSPAN:** 22.50m (73ft 10in)
**LENGTH:** 16m (52ft 6in)
**HEIGHT:** 4.85m (15ft 11in)
**ARMAMENT:** one 12.7mm (0.5in) trainable machine gun in dorsal turret, one 7.7mm (0.303in) machine gun in nose position, one 7.7mm (0.303in) machine gun in ventral position, one 7.7mm (0.303in) machine gun in tail position and one 7.7mm (0.303in) machine gun in each beam position, plus a bomb load of 1000kg (2205lb)

# Mitsubishi Ki-30 'Ann'

This aeroplane was the Imperial Japanese Army Air Force's first operational warplane with a double-row radial piston engine, variable-pitch propeller, internal weapons bay and split flaps. However, despite these modern features, the Ki-30 was a basically undistinguished type that saw most of its service in the Chinese theatre, where lack of effective fighter opposition allowed it to operate generally without molestation. The origins of the type can be traced to the mid-1930s, when the Imperial Japanese Army Air Force launched an ambitious programme of expansion based on aircraft of Japanese design and manufacture. The first of 18 prototype and service trials aircraft flew in February 1937. There followed 686 production aircraft, of which the survivors were relegated to the crew training role from 1942. The aircraft shown here is a Ki-30 of the 2nd Chutai, 10th Hikosentai, Imperial Japanese Army air service in 1942.

## SPECIFICATIONS

**COUNTRY OF ORIGIN:** Japan
**TYPE**: two-seat light attack bomber
**POWERPLANT**: one 708kW (950hp) Nakajima Ha-5 Kai (Army Type: 97) 14-cylinder two-row radial engine
**PERFORMANCE**: maximum speed 432km/h (263mph); climb to 5000m (16,405ft) in 10 minutes 36 seconds; service ceiling 8570m (28,120ft); range 1700km (1056 miles)
**WEIGHTS**: empty 2230kg (4916lb); maximum take-off 3322kg (7324lb)
**WINGSPAN**: 14.55m (47ft 9in)
**LENGTH**: 10.34m (33ft 11in)
**HEIGHT**: 3.65m (12ft)
**ARMAMENT**: one 7.7mm (0.303in) fixed forward-firing machine gun in leading edge of the port wing and one 7.7mm (0.303in) trainable rearward-firing machine gun in the rear cockpit, plus an internal bomb load of 400kg (882lb)

# Mitsubishi Ki-67 Hiryu 'Peggy'

The Ki-67 Hiryu (Flying Dragon) was without doubt the finest bomber to see service with the Imperial Japanese Army or Imperial Japanese Navy Air Forces in World War II, for it combined high performance with good defensive firepower, adequate offensive weapon load and a structure that was sturdy and provided good protection for the crew and fuel supply. Mitsubishi submitted the winning design to a 1940 requirement and the flight of the first of 19 prototypes took place in in December 1942. Service entry of the Ki-67-I began in the summer of 1944 after a development programme that had been much protracted by the army's desire to develop the Hiryu in several variants exploiting its excellent performance and handling. Production totalled 698 aircraft, of which some were converted as explosives-laden *kamikaze* aircraft. Pictured is a Ki-67 of the Imperial Japanese Army Air Force.

## SPECIFICATIONS

**COUNTRY OF ORIGIN:** Japan
**TYPE:** (Ki-67-I) six/eight-seat 'heavy' (actually medium) bomber
**POWERPLANT:** two 1417kW (1900hp) Mitsubishi Ha-104 (Army Type: 4) 18-cylinder two-row radial engines
**PERFORMANCE:** maximum speed 537km/h (334mph); climb to 6000m (19,685ft) in 14 minutes 30 seconds; service ceiling 9470m (31,070ft); range 3800km (2361 miles)
**WEIGHTS:** empty 8649kg (19,068lb); maximum take-off 13,765kg (30,347lb)
**WINGSPAN:** 22.50m (73ft 10in)
**LENGTH:** 18.70m (61ft 4in)
**HEIGHT:** 7.70m (25ft 3in)
**ARMAMENT:** one 20mm (0.79in) trainable cannon in dorsal turret, two 12.7mm (0.5in) trainable rearward-firing machine guns in tail position, one 12.7mm (0.5in) trainable machine gun in nose position and one 12.7mm (0.5in) machine gun in each beam position, plus a bomb or torpedo load of 1070kg (2359lb)

# Nakajima B5N 'Kate'

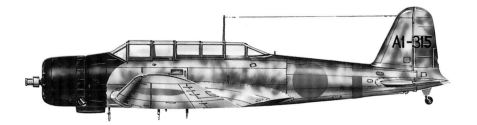

The B5N was the torpedo- and level bomber counterpart of the Aichi D3A dive-bomber and, as such, was a major weapon in the first part of the Japanese campaign in the Pacific theatre from December 1941. The type resulted from a 1934 requirement and the first of two prototypes flew in January 1937. Successful development paved the way for the B5N1 initial production model with the powerplant of one 626kW (840hp) Nakajima Hikari 3 radial engine. Production of the B5N1 bomber was complemented by that of its B5N1-K advanced trainer derivative and, by 1941, the type had been replaced in first-line service by the improved B5N2 with a more potent engine. B5N production totalled 1147 and the B5N2 remained in first-line service up to mid-1944, thereafter being retasked to less demanding roles such as maritime reconnaissance. Shown here is a B5N2 of the Imperial Japanese Navy Air Force, based on the fated carrier Akagi in 1941–42.

## SPECIFICATIONS

**COUNTRY OF ORIGIN:** Japan
**TYPE:** (B5N2) three-seat carrierborne and land-based torpedo- and level bomber
**POWERPLANT:** one 746kW (1000hp) Nakajima NK1B Sakae 11 nine-cylinder single- row radial engine
**PERFORMANCE:** maximum speed 378km/h (235mph); climb to 3000m (9845ft) in 7 minutes 40 seconds; service ceiling 8260m (27,100ft); range 1991km (1237 miles)
**WEIGHTS:** empty 2279kg (5024lb); maximum take-off 4100kg (9039lb)
**WINGSPAN:** 15.52 m (50ft 11in)
**LENGTH:** 10.30m (33ft 10in)
**HEIGHT:** 3.70m (12ft 2in)
**ARMAMENT:** one 7.7mm (0.303in) trainable rearward-firing machine gun in the rear cockpit, plus an external torpedo and bomb load of 800kg (1764lb)

# Nakajima B6N Tenzan 'Jill'

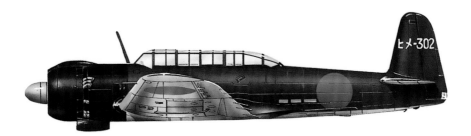

Designed to a 1939 requirement for a B5N successor, the B6N Tenzan (heavenly mountain) may be regarded as a extension of the design philosophy that inspired the B5N with considerably more power for significantly improved performance. The first of two prototypes flew in the spring of 1941, but the time needed to eradicate the problems that were encountered meant that the first of 133 B6N1 production aircraft entered service only late in 1943 with the 1394kW (1870hp) Nakajima NK7A Mamoru 11 radial engine. Further development of this engine was then cancelled, forcing Nakajima to develop the B6N2 with a different powerplant. Production of the B6N2 totalled 1133 aircraft in two subvariants, but little effective use could be made of these aircraft for lack of capable aircrew. The B6N3 was a purely land-based development that did not enter production. The aircraft pictured is a B6N2 of the Imperial Japanese Navy Air Force during 1944.

## SPECIFICATIONS

**COUNTRY OF ORIGIN:** Japan
**TYPE:** (B6N2) three-seat carrierborne and land-based torpedo bomber
**POWERPLANT:** one 1379kW (1850hp) Mitsubishi MK4T Kasei 25 14-cylinder two-row radial engine
**PERFORMANCE:** maximum speed 481km/h (299mph); climb to 5000m (16,405ft) in 10 minutes 24 seconds; service ceiling 9040m (29,660ft); range 3045km (1892 miles)
**WEIGHTS:** empty 3010kg (6636lb); maximum take-off 5650kg (12,456lb)
**WINGSPAN:** 14.89m (48ft 11in)
**LENGTH:** 10.87m (35ft 8in)
**HEIGHT:** 3.80m (12ft 6in)
**ARMAMENT:** one 7.7mm (0.303in) trainable rearward-firing machine gun in the rear of the cockpit and one 7.7mm (0.303in) trainable rearward-firing machine gun in the ventral tunnel position, plus an external torpedo and bomb load of 800kg (1764lb)

# Nakajima Ki-49 Donryu 'Helen'

The Donryu (Storm Dragon) was planned from 1938 as replacement for the Mitsubishi Ki-21, but proved so indifferent that it supplemented rather than replaced the older type. The first of three prototypes made its maiden flight in August 1939 and the evaluation of seven pre-production aircraft paved the way for the introduction from August 1941 of the Ki-49-I initial production variant, of which 129 were delivered with a powerplant of two 932kW (1250hp) Nakajima Ha-41 radial engines. There followed 667 examples of the Ki-49-II in two subvariants with an uprated and different powerplant, improved protection and heavier defensive firepower. There were also three prototypes of the Ki-58 escort derivative with no bombs, but a trainable armament of five 20mm (0.79in) cannon and three 12.7mm (0.5in) machine guns. The inability of the Ki-49 to fulfill its intended role meant that the aircraft was increasingly relegated to secondary duties in the later stages of the war.

## SPECIFICATIONS

**COUNTRY OF ORIGIN:** Japan

**TYPE:** (Ki-49-IIa) eight-seat 'heavy' (actually medium) bomber

**POWERPLANT:** two 1118kW (1500hp) Nakajima Ha-109 (Army Type 2) 14-cylinder two-row radial engines

**PERFORMANCE:** maximum speed 492km/h (306mph); climb to 5000m (16,405ft) in 13 minutes 39 seconds; service ceiling 9300m (30,510ft); range 2950km (1833 miles)

**WEIGHTS:** empty 6530kg (14,396lb); maximum take-off 11,400kg (25,133lb)

**WINGSPAN:** 20.42m (67ft)

**LENGTH:** 16.50m (54ft 2in)

**HEIGHT:** 4.25m (13ft 1in)

**ARMAMENT:** one 20mm (0.79in) trainable cannon in dorsal turret, one 12.7mm (0.5in) machine gun in nose position, one 12.7mm (0.5in) machine gun in tail position, one 12.7mm (0.5in) machine gun in ventral position and one 7.7mm (0.5in) machine gun in each beam position; bomb load of 1000kg (2205lb)

# North American B-25A/B Mitchell

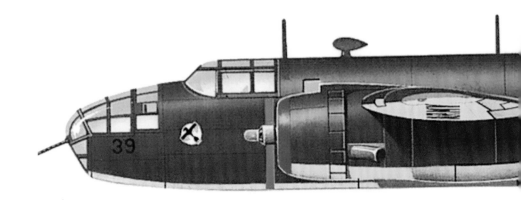

One of the most important US tactical warplanes of World War II and built to the extent of 9816 aircraft, the Mitchell was a classic medium bomber that was also developed into a potent anti-ship warplane. The origins of the type can be found in 1938, when North American gambled that the US Army Air Corps would need a new attack bomber. In response, work commenced on the NA-40 that first flew in January 1939 before conversion into the NA-40B to meet the definitive USAAC requirement issued in January 1939. The concept was then refined as the NA-62, subsequently ordered as 24 B-25 initial production aircraft which were delivered from February 1941. Later deliveries comprised 40 and 120 B-25A and B-25B aircraft, the former with self-sealing fuel tanks and the latter with dorsal and ventral turrets but no tail gun position. The B-25B was used in the 'Doolittle raid' of April 1942, when 16 aircraft lifted off from an aircraft carrier to bomb Tokyo.

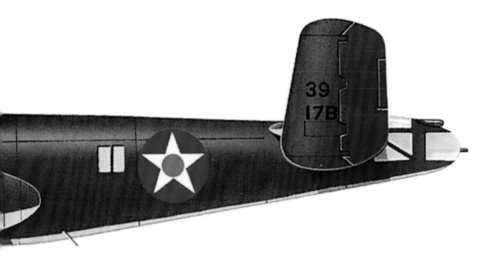

## SPECIFICATIONS

**COUNTRY OF ORIGIN:** United States

**TYPE:** (B-25B) five-seat medium bomber

**POWERPLANT:** two 1267kW (1700hp) Wright R-2600-9 14-cylinder two-row radial engines

**PERFORMANCE:** maximum speed 483km/h (300mph); service ceiling of 7175m (23,500ft); range 2172km (1350 miles) with a 1361kg (3000lb) bomb load

**WEIGHTS:** empty 9072kg (20,000lb); maximum take-off 12,909kg (28,460lb)

**WINGSPAN:** 30.66m (67ft 7in)

**LENGTH:** 16.13 m (52ft 11in)

**HEIGHT:** 4.80m (15ft 9in)

**ARMAMENT:** one 7.62mm (0.3in) trainable forward-firing machine gun in the nose position, two 12.7mm (0.5in) trainable machine guns in the dorsal turret and two 12.7mm (0.5in) trainable machine guns in the ventral turret, plus an internal bomb load of 1361kg (3000lb)

# North American B-25C/D Mitchell

The B-25 series entered combat service in 1942. Some early concerns were expressed by pilots regarding the type's often tricky handling qualities, but these were soon dispelled and the aircraft began to make a notable impact on the air war. The B-25B was followed into service by the virtually identical B-25C and B-25D. These were actually the first variants to enter large-scale production in the form of 1619 Inglewood-built B-25C and 2290 Kansas City-built B-25D machines with an uprated powerplant, an autopilot, external hardpoints for one 907kg (2000lb) torpedo or eight 113kg (250lb) bombs, provision for forward-firing machine guns in packs scabbed onto the sides of the forward fuselage and, in later aircraft, increased fuel capacity. The two models were used in most American theatres, and 533 B-25C/D aircraft were delivered to the UK as Mitchell Mk II aircraft to supplement 23 Mitchell Mk I (B-25B) machines.

## SPECIFICATIONS

**COUNTRY OF ORIGIN:** United States
**TYPE:** (B-25C) five-seat medium bomber
**POWERPLANT:** two 1267.5kW (1700hp) Wright R-2600-13 18-cylinder two-row radial engines
**PERFORMANCE:** maximum speed 457km/h (284mph); climb to 4570m (15,000ft) in 16 minutes 30 seconds; service ceiling 6460m (21,200ft); range 2454km (1525 miles) with a 1452kg (3200lb) bomb load
**WEIGHTS:** empty 9208kg (20,300lb); maximum take-off 18,960kg (41,800lb)
**WINGSPAN:** 20.60m (67ft 7in)
**LENGTH:** 16.12m (52ft 11in)
**HEIGHT:** 4.82m (15ft 10in)
**ARMAMENT:** two 12.7mm (0.5in) trainable forward-firing machine guns in the nose position, two 12.7mm (0.5in) trainable machine guns in the dorsal turret and two 12.7mm (0.5in) trainable machine guns in the ventral turret, plus an internal and external bomb and torpedo load of 1361kg (3000lb)

# North American B-25G/H/J Mitchell

**D**elivered to the extent of 405 aircraft including five B-25C conversions, the B-25G was a dedicated anti-ship model evolved for use in the Pacific theatre with a four-man crew and a 75mm (2.95in) M4 gun in the nose, together with two 12.7mm (0.5in) Browning fixed forward-firing machine guns and four 'package' guns. The 1000 examples of the B-25H had a lighter 75mm (2.95in) gun, eight 12.7mm (0.5in) fixed forward-firing machine guns, six 12.7mm (0.5in) trainable machine guns and provision for eight 127mm (5in) rockets under the wings. The 4318 examples of the B-25J had no 75mm (2.95in) gun and either a glazed B-25D nose or, in later aircraft, a 'solid' nose with eight 12.7mm (0.5in) guns. Some 313 B-25Js were delivered to the UK as Mitchell Mk III aircraft. The aircraft was exported widely and continued in service well after the war. The USAF retired its last B-25 staff transport in May 1960.

## SPECIFICATIONS

**COUNTRY OF ORIGIN:** United States
**TYPE:** (B-25H) five-seat medium bomber
**POWERPLANT:** two 1267.5kW (1700hp) Wright R-2600-13 18-cylinder two-row radial engines
**PERFORMANCE:** maximum speed 442km/h (275mph); climb to 4570m (15,000ft) in 19 minutes; service ceiling 7255m (23,800ft); range 4345km (2700 miles)
**WEIGHTS:** empty 9061kg (19,975lb); maximum take-off 16,351kg (36,047lb)
**WINGSPAN:** 20.6m (67ft 7in)
**LENGTH:** 15.7m (51ft 4in)
**HEIGHT:** 4.8m (15ft 9in)
**ARMAMENT:** one 75mm (2.95in) forward-firing gun in port lower side of nose, four 12.7mm (0.5in) machine guns in forward fuselage, two 12.7mm (0.5in) machine guns in dorsal turret, two 12.7mm (0.5in) trainable machine guns in tail position and one 12.7mm (0.5in) machine gun in each beam position; internal load of 2449kg (5400lb)

# North American P-51A /C Mustang

The Mustang was the finest all-round fighter of World War II, for it was a truly superb warplane that combined phenomenal performance, good acceleration, very good manoeuvrability, an extremely sturdy airframe and other operationally significant attributes in an aesthetically attractive package whose totality somehow seemed to be greater than the sum of its parts. The Mustang resulted from a British requirement and first flew in October 1940 with the Allison V-1710 engine, which was also used in the 1045 examples of the P-51 and P-51A (Mustang Mks I and II) that served from April 1942 in the low-level fighter and reconnaissance fighter roles. The P-51B and P-51C (1988 and 1750 aircraft respectively) then switched to the Packard V-1650 American-made version of a classic British engine, the Rolls-Royce Merlin. This transformed the Mustang from a mediocre aircraft into one of the most important fighters of World War II.

## SPECIFICATIONS

**COUNTRY OF ORIGIN:** United States
**TYPE:** (P-51B) single-seat fighter and fighter-bomber
**POWERPLANT:** one 1044kW (1400hp) Packard V-1650-3 12-cylinder Vee engine
**PERFORMANCE:** maximum speed 708km/h (440mph); climb to 3050m (10,000ft) in 1 minute 48 seconds; service ceiling 12,800m (42,000ft); range 3540km (2,200 miles)
**WEIGHTS:** empty 3103kg (6840lb); maximum take-off 5080kg (11,200lb)
**WINGSPAN:** 11.89m (37ft)
**LENGTH:** 9.83m (32ft 3in)
**HEIGHT:** 2.64m (8ft 8in)
**ARMAMENT:** six 12.7mm (0.5in) fixed forward-firing machine guns in the leading edges of the wing, plus an external bomb load of 907kg (2000lb)

# Northrop A-17

The A-17 was a development of the Gamma 2 transport for the attack role and the first of 110 A-17 aircraft was delivered in July 1935. There followed 129 examples of the A-17A with an uprated engine and retractable landing gear, plus two examples of the A-17AS three-seat command transport. All the American aircraft had been relegated to second-line tasks before the US's entry into World War II, but a number of aircraft (built as DB-8s after Douglas's take-over of Northrop) were exported and some of these played a more active role. The exports included 102 (including licence-built) aircraft for Sweden as well as 17, 20, 36 and 10 for Iraq, the Netherlands, Norway and Peru respectively. Peru also ordered 34 other aircraft that were impressed for US service as A-33s. These aircraft were armed with six 7.62mm (0.3in) machine guns and had a potential bomb load of 816kg (1800lb). France and the UK received 32 and 61 aircraft respectively.

## SPECIFICATIONS

**COUNTRY OF ORIGIN:** United States

**TYPE:** (A-17A) two-seat attack warplane

**POWERPLANT:** one 615kW (825hp) Pratt & Whitney R-1535-13 14-cylinder two-row radial engine

**PERFORMANCE:** maximum speed 354km/h (220mph); climb to 1525m (5000ft) in 3 minutes 54 seconds; service ceiling 5915m (19,400ft); range 1923km (1195 miles)

**WEIGHTS:** empty 2316kg (5106lb); maximum take-off 3425kg (7550lb)

**WINGSPAN:** 14.55m (47ft 9in)

**LENGTH:** 9.65m (31ft 8in)

**HEIGHT:** 3.66m (12ft)

**ARMAMENT:** four 7.62mm (0.3in) fixed forward-firing machine guns in leading edges of the wing and one 7.62mm (0.3in) trainable rearward-firing machine in the rear of the cockpit with provision for its use in the ventral hatch position, plus an internal and external bomb load of 544kg (1200lb)

# Northrop N-3PB

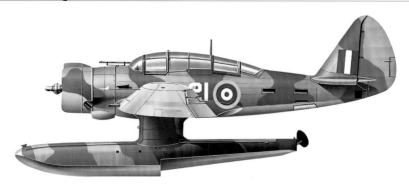

The N-3PB clearly owed much to the cantilever low-wing monoplanes that 'Jack' Northrop had designed while part of the Douglas Aircraft Company. In 1940, a Norwegian purchasing commission placed an order for 24 of the floatplanes, but shortly after this the Germans invaded the country and soon overran it. The Norwegian government-in-exile maintained its order for the N-3PB and the first example flew in January 1941. By April 1941, all the aircraft had been delivered to 'Little Norway', the Norwegian base area in Canada. One squadron operated the type, flying 18 of the floatplanes from three bases in Iceland on convoy escort patrols under the auspices of an RAF unit. By the summer of 1942, it was clear that the N-3PB was unsuitable for the task and the aircraft were relegated to the training role. Pictured here is an N3-PB of the Royal Norwegian Naval Air Service, operating as No. 330 Squadron RAF Coastal Command during 1941–42.

## SPECIFICATIONS

**COUNTRY OF ORIGIN:** United States

**TYPE:** (N-3PB) three-seat coastal reconnaissance and convoy escort floatplane

**POWERPLANT:** one 820kW (1100hp) Wright GR-1820-G205A Cyclone nine-cylinder single-row radial engine

**PERFORMANCE:** maximum speed 414km/h (257mph); climb to 4570m (15,000ft) in 14 minutes 24 seconds; service ceiling 7315m (24,000ft); range 1609km (1000 miles)

**WEIGHTS:** empty 2808kg (6190lb); maximum take-off 4808kg (10,600lb)

**WINGSPAN:** 14.91m (48ft 11in)

**LENGTH:** 10.97m (36ft)

**HEIGHT:** 3.66m (12ft)

**ARMAMENT:** four 12.7mm (0.5in) fixed forward-firing machine guns in leading edges of wing, one 7.62mm (0.3in) machine gun in rear of cockpit and one 7.62mm (0.3in) machine gun in ventral position, plus a load of 907kg (2000lb)

# Petlyakov Pe-2

The Pe-2 may be regarded as the Soviet counterpart of the de Havilland Mosquito and Junkers Ju 88, but it differed from its British and German counterparts in being optimized for the purely tactical role in a host of variants that were built to the extent of 11,427 aircraft. The origins of the design can be found in the VI-100 prototype for a high-altitude fighter that flew in 1939–40, but the design was then revised as the PB-100 dive-bomber with three rather than two crew members in unpressurized accommodation, a powerplant optimized for lower-altitude operations and different armament, including a lower-fuselage bomb bay. The PB-100 prototype was a conversion of the second VI-100 and first flew in June 1940. Later in the same month, the decision was taken for the PB-100 to be placed in immediate production with a number of minor changes as the Pe-2. This proved to be the outstanding Soviet tactical bomber of World War II.

## SPECIFICATIONS

**COUNTRY OF ORIGIN:** Soviet Union
**TYPE:** (Pe-2) three-seat multi-role attack bomber
**POWERPLANT:** two 820kW (1100hp) Klimov VK-105RA 12-cylinder Vee engines
**PERFORMANCE:** maximum speed 540km/h (335mph); climb to 5000m (16,405ft) in 7 minutes; service ceiling 8800m (28,870ft); range 1500km (932 miles) with a 2205lb (1000kg) bomb load
**WEIGHTS:** empty 5870kg (12,943lb); maximum take-off 8495kg (18,728lb)
**WINGSPAN:** 17.16m (56ft 4in)
**LENGTH:** 12.66m (41ft 7in)
**HEIGHT:** 4.00m (13ft 2in)
**ARMAMENT:** two 7.62mm (0.3in) fixed forward-firing machine guns in the nose, one 7.62mm (0.3in) trainable rearward-firing machine gun in the dorsal position and one 7.62mm (0.3in) trainable rearward-firing machine gun in the ventral position, plus an internal and external bomb load of 1600kg (3527lb)

# Petlyakov Pe-2FT

The original version of the Pe-2 was supplanted from the spring of 1942 by the Pe-2FT that featured improved defensive armament (single 7.62mm/0.3in) machine guns in a dorsal turret and either of two beam positions), removal of the underwing dive brakes, reduction of the nose glazing and, as availability permitted from February 1943, an uprated powerplant. Further development resulted in operational models such as the Pe-2R long-range photo-reconnaissance model with greater fuel capacity, the Pe-2UT dual-control trainer with a revised cockpit, and the Pe-3 multi-purpose fighter with a fixed forward-firing armament of two 20mm (0.79in) cannon and two 12.7mm (0.5in) machine guns, single 12.7mm (0.5in) trainable machine guns in the dorsal and ventral positions and underwing provision for 132mm (5.2in) rockets, plus many experimental developments. Pictured is a Pe-2FT of the Soviet Air Force, operating over the Eastern Front during World War II.

## SPECIFICATIONS

**COUNTRY OF ORIGIN:** Soviet Union
**TYPE:** (Pe-2FT) three-seat multi-role attack bomber
**POWERPLANT:** two 939.5kW (1260hp) Klimov VK-105PF 12-cylinder Vee engines
**PERFORMANCE:** maximum speed 580km/h (360mph); climb to 5000m (16,405ft) in 9 minutes 18 seconds; service ceiling 8800m (28,870ft); range 1315km (817 miles) with a 1000kg (2205lb) bomb load
**WEIGHTS:** empty 5950kg (13,119lb); maximum take-off 8520kg (18,783lb)
**WINGSPAN:** 17.11m (56ft 2in)
**LENGTH:** 12.78m (41ft 11in)
**HEIGHT:** 3.42m (11ft 3in)
**ARMAMENT:** two 7.62mm (0.3in) or one 7.62mm (0.3in) and one 12.7mm (0.5in) fixed forward-firing machine guns in nose, one 7.62mm (0.3in) machine gun in dorsal turret, one 7.62mm (0.3in) or 12.7mm (0.5in) trainable machine gun in ventral position and one 7.62mm (0.3in) or 12.7mm (0.5in) trainable lateral-firing machine gun in window positions, plus a bomb load of 1600kg (3527lb)

# Plage & Laskiewicz (Lublin) R-XVI

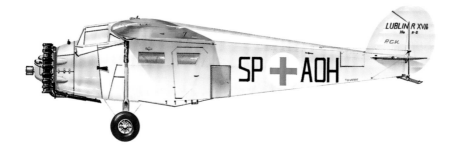

First flown early in 1932, the R-XVI prototype was a high-wing light transport with accommodation for four passengers and a single engine (a licence-built Wright Whirlwind by Skoda) driving a fixed-pitch propeller. This machine proved unsuitable for service with the national carrier LOT and was later taken in hand for modification with a strengthened fuselage revised internally for service as an air ambulance. Successful testing of the prototype at a medical aviation congress held in Spain in 1933 led to an order. There followed five examples of the R-XVIB production model with a variable-pitch propeller, an enclosed cockpit and a further modified fuselage. All six aircraft were still in service with the Polish air force at the time of the German invasion that started World War II in September 1939, and were used only for the casualty evacuation role during this campaign. None of the aircraft survived the war.

## SPECIFICATIONS

**COUNTRY OF ORIGIN:** Poland

**TYPE:** (R-XVIB) three-seat air ambulance, light transport and communications aeroplane

**POWERPLANT:** one 164kW (220hp) Skoda-built Wright Whirlwind J-5 seven-cylinder single-row radial engine

**PERFORMANCE:** maximum speed 190km/h (118mph); climb to 1000m (3280ft) in 6 minutes 30 seconds; service ceiling 4460m (14,635ft); range 800km (497 miles)

**WEIGHTS:** empty 1150kg (2535lb); normal take-off 1630kg (3593lb)

**WINGSPAN:** 14.93m (49ft)

**LENGTH:** 10.08m (33ft 1in)

**HEIGHT:** 2.96m (9ft 9in)

**ARMAMENT:** n/a

# Potez 63.11

In 1934, the French air ministry issued a complex requirement for a multi-role warplane to be powered by two examples of the new small-diameter radial engines developed by Gnome-Rhòne and Hispano-Suiza, to carry a fixed forward-firing armament that included at least one 20mm (0.79in) cannon, to carry sufficient radio equipment for the type to operate as a controller for single-seat fighters in running engagements with bomber formations and to possess the capability for operation in three fighter roles. The winning design was the Potez 63, which was then developed in a number of forms including the Potez 63.11 for tactical reconnaissance and army co-operation. First flown in December 1938, the Potez 63.11 entered service in November of the same year and about 925 Potez 63.11A.3 aircraft had been delivered by June 1940. After this, the type was operated by both the Free French and Vichy French forces in North Africa and the Middle East.

## SPECIFICATIONS

**COUNTRY OF ORIGIN:** France
**TYPE:** three-seat multi-role warplane
**POWERPLANT:** two 522kW (700hp) Gnome-Rhòne 14M-4/5 radial engines
**PERFORMANCE:** maximum speed 425km/h (264mph); climb to 3000m (9845ft) in 6 minutes; service ceiling 8500m (27,885ft); range 1500km (932 miles)
**WEIGHTS:** empty 3135kg (6911lb); maximum take-off 4530kg (9987lb)
**WINGSPAN:** 16m (52ft 6in)
**LENGTH:** 10.93m (35ft 11in)
**HEIGHT:** 3.08m (10ft 1in)
**ARMAMENT:** one 7.5mm (0.29in) machine gun under central fuselage, one 7.5mm (0.29in) machine gun in rear fuselage and one 7.5mm (0.29in) machine gun in the rear cockpit, or in some aircraft three 7.5mm (0.29in) machine guns in nose and under fuselage, four 7.5mm (0.29in) machine guns in two two-gun underwing packs, three 7.5mm (0.29in) machine guns under fuselage and two 7.5mm (0.29in) machine guns in cockpit; external bomb load of 300kg (661lb)

# Potez 633

Resulting from a 1934 requirement for a multi-role warplane, the Potez 630 paved the way for a number of role-optimized variants. One of the first was a light bomber, which was evaluated from January 1937 as the Potez 632.01 prototype conversion of the Potez 630.02 night-fighter and, in May 1938, an order was placed for 125 examples (only six delivered) of the Potez 633B.2 production version that was basically similar to the Potez 631C.3 fighter except for its accommodation, armament and the reintroduction of a glazed lower nose to provide a bombardier position. Other sales were made to China, Greece, Romania and Switzerland and 30 of these aircraft were retained for French service. Another model was the Potez 637A.3 (60 delivered) three-seat attack and reconnaissance model with a ventral gondola and heavier armament. Pictured is one 21 aircraft supplied to Romania, which were used in the German campaign in the Ukraine.

## SPECIFICATIONS

**COUNTRY OF ORIGIN:** France
**TYPE:** (Potez 633B.2) two-seat light bomber
**POWERPLANT:** two 522kW (700hp) Gnome-Rhòne 14M-6/7 14-cylinder two-row radial engines
**PERFORMANCE:** maximum speed 439km/h (273mph); climb to 4000m (13,125ft) in 8 minutes 30 seconds; service ceiling 8000m (26,250ft); range 1300km (808 miles)
**WEIGHTS:** empty 2450kg (5401lb); maximum take-off 4500kg (9921lb)
**WINGSPAN:** 16m (52ft 6in)
**LENGTH:** 11.07m (36ft 4in)
**HEIGHT:** 3.62m (11ft 11in)
**ARMAMENT:** one 7.5mm (0.29in) fixed forward-firing machine gun in the upper starboard side of the forward fuselage and one 7.5mm (0.29in) trainable rearward-firing machine gun in the rear cockpit, plus an internal bomb load of 400kg (882lb)

# PZL P.23 Karas

Stemming from the P.13 project for a six-passenger transport, the P.23 Karas (Crucian Carp) was a light bomber and army co-operation warplane. The P.23/I Karas was the first of three prototypes and flew in August 1934. A number of problems had to be overcome before the type was ordered into production as the P.23A trainer with the 440kW (590hp) Pegasus IIM2 engine and P.23B operational model with an uprated engine (40 and 210 aircraft respectively). With their fixed landing gear, indifferent performance, poor armament and cramped accommodation, the aircraft suffered very heavy losses in the German invasion of September 1939, before 31 survivors were flown to Romania. Another 54 aircraft were delivered to Bulgaria in two P.43 variants with Gnome-Rhòne radial engines. Pictured is a P.23B operated by No 42 Squadron, Polish Air Force attached to the Pomorze Army in September 1939.

## SPECIFICATIONS

**COUNTRY OF ORIGIN:** Poland

**TYPE:** (P.23B Karas) three-seat light reconnaissance bomber

**POWERPLANT:** one 507kW (680hp) PZL (Bristol) Pegasus VIII nine-cylinder single-row radial engine

**PERFORMANCE:** maximum speed 300km/h (186mph); climb to 2000m (6560ft) in 4 minutes 45 seconds; service ceiling 7300m (23,950ft); range 1400km (870 miles)

**WEIGHTS:** empty 1928kg (4250lb); maximum take-off 3526kg (7773lb)

**WINGSPAN:** 13.95m (45ft 9in)

**LENGTH:** 9.68m (31ft 9in)

**HEIGHT:** 3.30m (10ft 10in)

**ARMAMENT:** one 7.7mm (0.303in) fixed forward-firing machine gun in the forward fuselage, one 7.7mm (0.303in) trainable rearward-firing machine gun with 600 rounds in the rear cockpit and one 7.7mm (0.303in) machine gun in the ventral position, plus an external bomb load of 700kg (1543lb)

# Savoia-Marchetti SM.79 Sparviero

**A**rguably one of the finest torpedo bombers of World War II, the Sparviero (Sparrowhawk) was notable for its three-engined layout and 'hunchback' fuselage. First flown in 1934 as the SM.79P civil transport prototype with eight-passenger seating, the type was then developed as a medium reconnaissance bomber and entered service as the SM.79-I with the uprated powerplant of three Alfa Romeo 126 radial engines and a large ventral gondola. The following SM.79-II was optimized for the anti-ship role with two 450mm (17.72in) torpedoes and a powerplant of three 746kW (1000hp) Piaggio P.XI RC.40 or 768kW (1030hp) Fiat A.80 RC.41 radial engines. The final Italian model was the SM.79-III improved SM.79-II with heavier defensive armament, but no ventral gondola. Deliveries totalled 1230 aircraft. The aircraft continued in service after World War II as a transport with the Aeronautica Militare Italiana.

## SPECIFICATIONS

**COUNTRY OF ORIGIN:** Italy
**TYPE:** (SM.79-I) four/five-seat medium reconnaissance bomber
**POWERPLANT:** three 582kW (780hp) Alfa Romeo 126 RC.34 9-cylinder single-row radial engines
**PERFORMANCE:** maximum speed 430km/h (267mph); climb to 5000m (16,405ft) in 19 minutes 45 seconds; service ceiling 6500m (21,325ft); range 1900km (1181 miles) with a 1250kg (2756lb) bomb load
**WEIGHTS:** empty 6800kg (14,991lb); maximum take-off 10,480kg (23,104lb)
**WINGSPAN:** 21.20m (69ft 3in)
**LENGTH:** 15.62m (51ft 3in)
**HEIGHT:** 4.40m (14ft 5in)
**ARMAMENT:** one 12.7mm (0.5in) fixed forward-firing machine gun above cockpit, one 12.7mm (0.5in) trainable rearward-firing machine gun in dorsal position, one 12.7mm (0.5in) machine gun in ventral position and one 7.7mm (0.303in) machine gun in two beam positions; bomb load of 2756lb (1250kg)

# SM.79B, JR and K Sparviero

The SM.79 was exported in a number of twin-engined forms. The SM.79B was the SM.79-I version for Brazil (three machines) with 694kW (930hp) Alfa Romeo 128 RC.18 engines, Iraq (four machines) with 768kW (1030hp) Fiat A.80 RC.41 engines and Romania (24 machines) with 746kW (1000hp) Gnome-Rhône 14K Mistral-Major engines, while the SM.79JR was another model for Romania (40 machines), similar to the SM.79B, with 835kW (1120hp) Junkers Jumo 211Da engines. Sixteen of the latter were built under licence. The last export model was the SM.79K version of the SM.79-I for Yugoslavia (45 machines). Italian variants were the SM.79C VIP transport conversions of 16 SM.79-Is with 746kW (1000hp) Piaggio P.XI RC.40 engines and no dorsal or ventral gun positions and the SM.79T long-range version of the SM.79C with 582kW (780hp) Alfa Romeo 126 RC.34 engines and significantly increased fuel capacity.

## SPECIFICATIONS

**COUNTRY OF ORIGIN:** Italy
**TYPE:** (SM.79JR) four/five-seat medium reconnaissance bomber
**POWERPLANT:** two 835kW (1120hp) Junkers Jumo 211Da 12-cylinder inverted-Vee engines
**PERFORMANCE:** maximum speed 445km/h (276mph); climb to 3000m (9845ft) in 8 minutes 36 seconds; service ceiling 7400m (24,280ft)
**WEIGHTS:** empty 7185kg (15,840lb); maximum take-off 10,775kg (23,754lb)
**WINGSPAN:** 21.20m (69ft 3in)
**LENGTH:** 16.10m (52ft 10in)
**HEIGHT:** 4.40m (14ft 5in)
**ARMAMENT:** one 13mm (0.51in) fixed forward-firing machine gun above the cockpit, one 13mm (0.51in) trainable rearward-firing machine gun in the dorsal position, one 13mm (0.51in) trainable rearward-firing machine gun in the ventral position and one 7.92mm (0.31in) machine gun in either of the two beam positions, plus an internal bomb load of 1250kg (2756lb)

# Savoia-Marchetti SM.81 Pipistrello

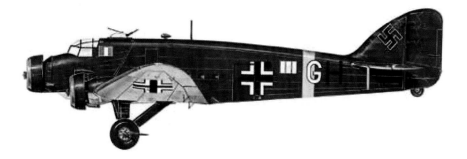

**D**eveloped in parallel with the SM.73 transport, with which it shared a basically common airframe, the Pipistrello (Bat) was a dual-role bomber and transport that first flew in 1934 and entered service in 1935. The SM.81 was built to the extent of 535 aircraft in three subvariants that differed only in their powerplants, which could comprise any of three types of radial engine (two Italian and one French, the last from captured stocks). The SM.81 saw extensive service in the Italian conquest of Abyssinia in the mid-1930s and still proved moderately effective in the early part of the Spanish Civil War, but from the time of Italy's June 1940 entry into World War II was used increasingly in the dedicated transport role, although it did undertake night bombing raids in North Africa. The type survived the war in modest numbers and remained in Italian service to 1950. Pictured here is an SM.81 of the Gruppo Transporti 'Terraciano', air force of the Repubblica Sociale Italiana.

## SPECIFICATIONS

**COUNTRY OF ORIGIN:** Italy
**TYPE:** (SM.81) five/six-seat bomber and transport
**POWERPLANT:** three 499.5kW (670hp) Piaggio P.X RC.35 nine-cylinder single-row radial engines, or 485kW (650hp) Alfa Romeo 125 RC.35 or 126 RC.34 nine-cylinder single-row radial engines, or 485kW (650hp) Gnome- Rhòne 14-K 14-cylinder two-row radial engines
**PERFORMANCE:** maximum speed 340km/h (211mph); climb to 3000m (9845ft) in 12 minutes; service ceiling 7000m (22,965ft); range 2000km (1243 miles)
**WEIGHTS:** empty 6300kg (13,889lb); maximum take-off 10,055kg (22,167lb)
**WINGSPAN:** 24m (78ft 9in)
**LENGTH:** 17.80m (58ft 5in)
**HEIGHT:** 6m (19ft 8in)
**ARMAMENT:** two 7.7mm (0.303in) or one 12.7mm (0.5in) machine guns in dorsal turret, two 7.7mm (0.303in) machine guns in ventral turret and one 7.7mm (0.303in) machine gun in beam positions, plus an internal bomb load of 4409lb (2000kg)

# Short Singapore

In 1926, Short produced the Singapore Mk I twin-engine flying boat that was built only in prototype form and, in 1931, developed this into the Singapore Mk II with a four-engine powerplant comprising two tandem pairs of tractor/pusher engines. The Singapore Mk II showed considerable promise and, in May 1934, the Air Ministry ordered four development machines, of which the first flew in July of the same year and soon received the designation Singapore Mk III. This paved the way for a further 33 boats and all 37 machines had been delivered by June 1937 for use by five squadrons. The type was relegated to Far Eastern service in 1940–41 and, in December 1941, the last four boats were handed over to the Royal New Zealand Air Force for continued service into 1942. Pictured here is one of the Mk III aircraft on the strength of No 203 Squadron, RAF, based at the British Middle East outpost of Aden in 1940.

## SPECIFICATIONS

**COUNTRY OF ORIGIN:** United Kingdom
**TYPE:** (Singapore Mk III) eight-seat maritime reconnaissance flying boat
**POWERPLANT:** four 455kW (610hp) Rolls-Royce Kestrel VIII/XX 12-cylinder Vee engines
**PERFORMANCE:** maximum speed 219km/h (136mph); climb to 1525m (5000ft) in 7 minutes; service ceiling 4510m (14,800ft); range 1987 km (1235 miles)
**WEIGHTS:** empty 9237kg (20,364lb); maximum take-off 14,692kg (32,390lb)
**WINGSPAN:** 27.43m (90ft)
**LENGTH:** 19.56m (64ft 2in)
**HEIGHT:** 7.19m (23ft 7in)
**ARMAMENT:** one 7.7mm (0.303in) trainable forward-firing machine gun in bow position, one 7.7mm (0.303in) trainable rearward-firing machine gun in dorsal position and one 7.7mm (0.303in) trainable rearward-firing machine gun in tail position, plus a bomb load of 590kg (1300lb)

# Short Stirling Mks I to V

The first four-engine heavy bomber to enter service with Bomber Command of the Royal Air Force during World War II, the Stirling was also the only British four-engined bomber to enter service after having been designed wholly as such, for the Avro Lancaster and Handley Page Halifax were both four-engined developments of two-engined designs. Even so, the Stirling was a workman-like rather than inspired aeroplane largely as a result of the Air Ministry's demand for a span of less than 30.48m (100ft). The Stirling Mk I entered service in August 1940 and production of 2374 aircraft included 756 Mk I bombers with 1189kW (1595hp) Hercules XI engines, 875 Mk III bombers with a revised dorsal turret, 579 Mk IV paratroop and glider-towing aircraft without nose and dorsal turrets and 160 Mk V unarmed transports. Pictured here is a Mk V of No 196 Squadron, RAF, based at Sheperd's Grove in the United Kingdom during 1946.

## SPECIFICATIONS

**COUNTRY OF ORIGIN:** United Kingdom
**TYPE:** (Stirling Mk III) seven/eight-seat heavy bomber
**POWERPLANT:** four 1230kW (1650hp) Bristol Hercules XVI 14-cylinder two-row radial engines
**PERFORMANCE:** maximum speed 434km/h (270mph); initial climb rate 244m (800ft) per minute; service ceiling 5180m (17,000ft); range 3235km (2010 miles) with a 1588kg (3500lb) bomb load
**WEIGHTS:** empty 21,274kg (46,900lb); maximum take-off 31,752kg (70,000lb)
**WINGSPAN:** 30.20m (99ft 1in)
**LENGTH:** 26.59m (87ft 3in)
**HEIGHT:** 6.93m (22ft 9in)
**ARMAMENT:** two 7.7mm (0.303in) trainable forward-firing machine guns in the nose turret, two 7.7mm (0.303in) trainable machine guns in the dorsal turret and four 7.7mm (0.303in) trainable rearward-firing machine guns in the tail turret, plus an internal bomb load of 6350kg (14,000lb)

# Short Sunderland Mk I

A 1933 requirement for a modern four-engined monoplane flying boat prompted designs from two companies including Short, which had an ideal starting point for its S.25 in the S.23 'Empire' class of civil flying boats. This proven lineage was a factor that contributed to the Air Ministry's order for 21 production examples of the S.25 in March 1936, some 18 months before the first prototype made its maiden flight in October 1937. The initial production model was the Sunderland Mk I that entered service in the summer of 1938 with an initial two squadrons. By the time World War II started in September 1939, another two British-based squadrons had converted onto the type and the rising rate of production allowed another three to convert during the first months of the war. Sunderland Mk I production totalled 90 boats, 15 of them by the Blackburn Aircraft Company, all powered by 753kW (1010hp) Bristol Pegasus engines.

## SPECIFICATIONS

**COUNTRY OF ORIGIN:** United Kingdom
**TYPE:** (Sunderland Mk I) 10-seat maritime reconnaissance flying boat
**POWERPLANT:** four 753kW (1010hp) Bristol Pegasus XXII nine-cylinder single-row radial engines
**PERFORMANCE:** maximum speed 336km/h (209mph); climb to 1525m (5000ft) in 7 minutes 12 seconds; service ceiling 4570m (15,000ft); range 4023km (2500 miles)
**WEIGHTS:** empty 13,875kg (30,589lb); maximum take-off 22,226kg (49,000lb)
**WINGSPAN:** 34.38m (112ft 10in)
**LENGTH:** 26.00m (85ft 4in)
**HEIGHT:** 10.52m (34ft 6in)
**ARMAMENT:** two 7.7mm (0.303in) trainable forward-firing machine guns in bow turret, four 7.7mm (0.303in) trainable rearward-firing machine guns in tail turret and one 7.7mm (0.303in) machine gun in each beam position, plus an internal bomb, depth charge and mine load of 907kg (2000lb)

# Short Sunderland Mks II to V

The Sunderland Mk II first flew in August 1941 as a Mk I development with four 783kW (1050hp) Bristol Pegasus XVIII radial engines and, later in the production run of 58 such boats, the replacement of the single machine guns in the manually operated waist positions by two guns in a dorsal turret and the addition of air-to-surface search radar. First flown in June 1942, the Sunderland Mk III was the first major production model of the family and was in essence a late-production Sunderland Mk II with a revised planing bottom. Production of 407 such boats lasted to late 1943. The last production model was the Sunderland GR.Mk V, of which 143 were completed up to June 1946 with a significantly improved powerplant, better armament and detail modifications. The Mk III was converted for use as a long-range passenger aircraft and operated by BOAC from March 1943 on gradually extending routes.

## SPECIFICATIONS

**COUNTRY OF ORIGIN:** United Kingdom
**TYPE:** (Sunderland GR.Mk V) 10-seat maritime reconnaissance flying boat
**POWERPLANT:** four 895kW (1200hp) Pratt & Whitney R-1830-90B Twin Wasp 14-cylinder two-row radial engines
**PERFORMANCE:** maximum speed 343km/h (213mph); climb to 3660m (12,000ft) in 16 minutes; ceiling 5455m (17,900ft); range 2980 miles (4796km)
**WEIGHTS:** empty 16,738kg (36,900lb); maximum take-off 27,216kg (60,000lb)
**WINGSPAN:** 34.38m (112ft 10in)
**LENGTH:** 26.00m (85ft 4in)
**HEIGHT:** 10.52m (34ft 6in)
**ARMAMENT:** two 7.7mm (0.303in) machine guns in bow turret, provision for four 7.7mm (0.303in) machine guns on sides of bow, two 7.7mm (0.303in) machine guns in dorsal turret, four 7.7mm (0.303in) machine guns in tail turret and one 12.7mm (0.5in) machine gun in each beam positions, plus an internal bomb, depth charge and mine load of 4960lb (2250kg)

# Sukhoi Su-2

The Su-2 was designed in competition to the Ilyushin Il-2 as a means of providing the Soviet ground forces with potent close air support. Like the Il-2, therefore, the type's origins can be traced to the Soviet doctrine adopted in the mid-1930s that air power should be seen not as a means of projecting strategic capabilities deep into the enemy's rear areas and homeland, but as a tactical adjunct of the ground forces. Pavel Sukhoi had previously worked as head of one of the design brigades in the Tupolev Design Bureau, where his last task had been the development of the ANT-51 tactical reconnaissance and ground-attack monoplane and, on being allowed to establish his own design bureau, he set about the evolution of the ANT-51 into the BB-1 prototype, which entered production as the Su-2. Some 2000 aircraft were completed between 1940 and 1942, before this indifferent type was relegated to training use from 1943.

## SPECIFICATIONS

**COUNTRY OF ORIGIN:** Soviet Union
**TYPE:** two-seat light attack bomber and reconnaissance warplane
**POWERPLANT:** one 746kW (1000hp) Tumanskii M-88B 14-cylinder two-row radial engine
**PERFORMANCE:** maximum speed 460km/h (286mph); climb to 4000m (13,125ft) in 8 minutes 12 seconds; service ceiling 8800m (28,870ft); range 1200km (746 miles)
**WEIGHTS:** empty 2970kg (6548lb); maximum take-off 4375kg (9645lb)
**WINGSPAN:** 14.30m (46ft 11in)
**LENGTH:** 10.46m (34ft 4in)
**HEIGHT:**
**ARMAMENT:** between four and eight 7.62mm (0.3in) fixed forward-firing machine guns in the leading edges of the wings and one 7.62mm (0.3in) trainable rearward-firing machine gun in the dorsal turret, plus an internal and external bomb and rocket load of 900kg (1984lb)

# Supermarine Walrus

In 1920, Supermarine flew its Channel flying boat and, in 1922, the Seagull Mk I development of this machine. There followed a development programme that led in June 1933 to the Seagull Mk V that introduced a predominantly metal structure. The Australian government ordered 24 of this type and its success led to a British contract for 12 catapult-capable boats that received the revised designation Walrus Mk I in 1935. Later orders increased the total to 556 boats (the later examples with air-to-surface radar) for service with the Fleet Air Arm and Royal Air Force in the reconnaissance and air/sea rescue roles with the 473.5kW (635hp) Pegasus IIM2 engine. The final model, of which 191 were delivered up to January 1944, was the Walrus Mk II with an uprated engine and a wooden hull. Pictured here is a Walrus Mk I of No 700 Squadron, Fleet Air Arm, based on HMS Belfast in the early 1940s.

## SPECIFICATIONS

**COUNTRY OF ORIGIN:** United Kingdom

**TYPE:** (Walrus Mk II) four-seat coastal and shipborne air/sea rescue, spotter and anti-submarine amphibian flying boat

**POWERPLANT:** one 578kW (775hp) Bristol Pegasus VI nine-cylinder single-row radial engine

**PERFORMANCE:** maximum speed 217km/h (135mph); climb to 3050m (10,000ft) in 12 minutes 30 seconds; service ceiling 5640m (18,500ft); range 966 km (600 miles)

**WEIGHTS:** empty 2223kg (4900lb); maximum take-off 3334kg (7350lb)

**WINGSPAN:** 13.97m (45ft 10in)

**LENGTH:** 11.58m (38ft)

**HEIGHT:** 5.13m (16ft 11in) with the main landing gear units lowered

**ARMAMENT:** one 7.7mm (0.303in) trainable forward-firing machine gun in the bow position and one or two 7.7mm (0.303in) machine guns in the dorsal position, plus a bomb and depth charge load of 272kg (600lb)

# Tupolev SB-2

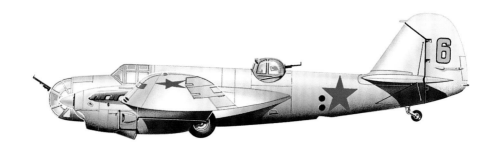

The SB-2 was almost certainly the most capable bomber serving anywhere in the world during the mid-1930s, in purely numerical terms was the most important bomber in the world during the late 1930s, and was also the first 'modern' aeroplane of the stressed-skin type to enter production in the Soviet Union, an event that took place in 1935. The SB-2 was initially delivered with 544kW (730hp) M-100 engines driving fixed-pitch propellers, but then came the 641kW (860hp) M-100A engine in a wider nacelle and driving a variable-pitch propeller. SB-2 series production totalled 6967 aircraft, the most important variant of which was the SB-2bis with uprated and different engines and greater fuel capacity. Other variants included 200 SB-RK dive-bombers with 820kW (1100hp) Klimov M-105R engines and the 111 Czechoslovak licence-built B 71 bombers. Pictured is an SB-2bis of the Red Air Force, captured by the Germans late in 1941.

## SPECIFICATIONS

**COUNTRY OF ORIGIN:**Soviet Union
**TYPE:** (SB-2bis) three-seat light bomber
**POWERPLANT:** two 716kW (960hp) Klimov M-103 12-cylinder Vee engines
**PERFORMANCE:** maximum speed 450km/h (280mph); climb to 1000m (3280ft) in 1 minute 48 seconds; service ceiling 9000m (29,530ft); range 2300km (1429 miles)
**WEIGHTS:** empty 4768kg (10,511lb); maximum take-off 7880kg (17,372lb)
**WINGSPAN:** 20.33m (66ft 9in)
**LENGTH:** 12.57m (41ft 3in)
**HEIGHT:** 3.25m (10ft 8in)
**ARMAMENT:** two 7.62mm (0.3in) trainable forward-firing machine guns in the nose position, one 7.62mm (0.3in) trainable rearward-firing machine gun in the dorsal turret and one 7.62mm (0.3in) trainable rearward-firing machine gun in the ventral position, plus an internal bomb load of 600kg (1323lb)

# Tupolev Tu-2

First flown in ANT-58 prototype form during January 1941, the Tu-2 was one of the best high-speed bombers to see service in World War II, but was built in larger numbers (2500 or more aircraft) after the end of the war than during the conflict. Developed via the ANT-59 and ANT-60 prototypes, then the Tu-2 pre-production model, the Tu-2S initial production model was delivered from the spring of 1944 as a Tu-2 development with uprated engines and heavier offensive and defensive armament. The type proved to possess excellent operational capabilities in terms of its performance, strength and versatility in the attack bomber and ground-attack roles. The only two other models to see significant combat service during World War II were the Tu-2D long-range model and the Tu-2R photo-reconnaissance model. The aircraft pictured is a Tu-2S of a Soviet bomber regiment operating on the Eastern Front in 1945.

## SPECIFICATIONS

**COUNTRY OF ORIGIN:** Soviet Union
**TYPE:** (Tu-2S) four-seat medium attack bomber
**POWERPLANT:** two 1379kW (1850hp) Shvetsov ASh-82FN 14-cylinder two-row radial engines
**PERFORMANCE:** maximum speed 547km/h (340mph); climb to 5000m (16,405ft) in 9 minutes 30 seconds; service ceiling 9500m (31,170ft); range 2100km (1305 miles)
**WEIGHTS:** empty 7474kg (16,477lb); maximum take-off 11,360kg (25,044lb)
**WINGSPAN:** 18.86m (61ft 11in)
**LENGTH:** 13.80m (45ft 3in)
**HEIGHT:** 4.56m (14ft 11in)
**ARMAMENT:** two 20mm (0.79in) fixed forward-firing cannon in wing roots, one 12.7mm (0.5in) trainable rearward-firing machine gun in rear of the cockpit, one 12.7mm (0.5in) machine gun in dorsal position and one 12.7mm (0.5in) machine gun in ventral position, plus an internal bomb load of 4000kg (8818lb)

# Vickers Vincent

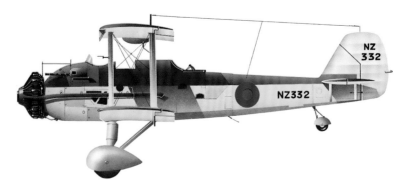

In the early 1930s, the standard army cooperation warplanes operated by the Royal Air Force in overseas theatres were the Fairey IIIF and Westland Wapiti. Both these types were obsolescent and, in its search for a successor type, the Air Ministry decided that the new Vildebeest torpedo bomber had the potential to be transformed into an effective general-purpose warplane. Therefore, in 1932, a Vildebeest Mk I was converted as prototype of a general-purpose version and successful evaluation of this conversion resulted in orders for 196 Vincent Mk Is completed between July 1934 and October 1936 as new aircraft or Vildebeest conversions. Some 171 of the aircraft served with the RAF (12 squadrons in India, the Middle East and East Africa), and they continued to serve in Iraq until 1941. Small numbers were transferred to Iraq and New Zealand. Pictured here is a Vincent of the Royal New Zealand Air Force in 1940.

## SPECIFICATIONS

**COUNTRY OF ORIGIN:** United Kingdom
**TYPE:** three-seat general-purpose warplane
**POWERPLANT:** one 473.5kW (635hp) Bristol Pegasus IIM3 nine-cylinder single-row radial engine
**PERFORMANCE:** maximum speed 228.5km/h (142mph); initial climb rate 233m (765ft ) per minute; service ceiling 5180m (17,000ft); range 2012km (1,250 miles)
**WEIGHTS:** empty 1918kg (4229lb); maximum take-off 3674kg (8100lb)
**WINGSPAN:** 14.94m (49ft)
**LENGTH:** 11.175m (36ft 8in)
**HEIGHT:** 5.41m (17ft 9in)
**ARMAMENT:** one 7.7mm (0.303in) fixed forward-firing machine gun in the port side of the forward fuselage and one 7.7mm (0.303in) trainable rearward-firing machine gun in the rear cockpit, plus an external bomb load of 499kg (1100lb)

# Vickers Wellesley

**D**esigned in 1933 as a private venture to meet an official requirement for a general-purpose and torpedo bomber, the Wellesley was based on the novel geodetic structure and emerged for its first flight in June 1935 as a fabric-covered cantilever monoplane with a wing of high aspect ratio. Such were the capabilities of the prototype that the Air Ministry ordered an initial 96 Wellesley Mk I aircraft optimized for the medium bomber role with its bombs carried in two panniers under the wing. The Wellesley Mk I entered service in April 1937 and production up to May 1938 and totalled 176 aircraft, most of the later aircraft being completed (with the unofficial designation Wellesley Mk II) with a continuous 'glasshouse' canopy bridging the front and rear cockpits. The Wellesley saw useful service in East and North Africa during the first part of World War II. Pictured is a Wellesley Mk I of No 76 Squadron, based at Finningley in 1938.

## SPECIFICATIONS

**COUNTRY OF ORIGIN:** United Kingdom
**TYPE:** (Wellesley Mk I) two/three-seat general-purpose bomber
**POWERPLANT:** one 622.5kW (835hp) Bristol Pegasus XX nine-cylinder single-row radial engine
**PERFORMANCE:** maximum speed 367km/h (228mph); climb to 6000m (19,685ft) in 17 minutes 30 seconds; service ceiling 7770m (25,500ft); range 4635km (2880 miles) with a 1060lb (481kg) bomb load
**WEIGHTS:** empty 3066kg (6760lb); maximum take-off 5670kg (12,500lb)
**WINGSPAN:** 22.73m (74ft 7in)
**LENGTH:** 11.66m (39ft 3in)
**HEIGHT:** 4.67m (15ft 4in)
**ARMAMENT:** one 7.7mm (0.303in) fixed forward-firing machine gun in the leading edge of the port wing and one 7.7mm (0.303in) trainable rearward-firing machine gun in the rear cockpit, plus an internal bomb load of 907kg (2000lb)

# Wellington B.Mks I to X

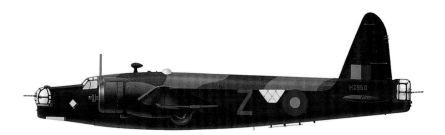

One of the most important warplanes in the British inventory at the beginning of World War II, the Wellington bore the brunt of the bomber effort until large numbers of four-engined heavy bombers became available in the later stages of 1941. The type then found an important second career in the maritime reconnaissance, transport and training roles until a time well after the end of the war. Total production was 11,461, the last machine not being delivered until October 1945. Entering service in October 1938, the initial model was the Wellington Mk I with 746kW (1000hp) Pegasus XVIII radial engines, and bomber development continued via the Mk III with Rolls-Royce Merlin Vee engines, Mk III with Hercules radial engines, Mk IV with Pratt & Whitney Twin Wasp radial engines, Mk VI with Merlin engines and Mk X with Hercules engines. Wellingtons formed the major component of the first 1000-bomber raid.

## SPECIFICATIONS

**COUNTRY OF ORIGIN:** United Kingdom
**TYPE:** (Wellington Mk X) six-seat medium bomber
**POWERPLANT:** two 1249kW (1675hp) Bristol Hercules XI or XVI 14-cylinder two-row radial engines
**PERFORMANCE:** maximum speed 410km/h (255mph); climb to 4570m (15,000ft) in 27 minutes 42 seconds; service ceiling 6705m (22,000ft); range 3033.5km (1885 miles) with a 680kg (1500lb) bomb load
**WEIGHTS:** empty 10,194kg (22,474lb); maximum take-off 16,556kg (36,500lb)
**WINGSPAN:** 26.26m (86ft 2in)
**LENGTH:** 19.68m (64ft 7in)
**HEIGHT:** 5.31m (17ft 5in)
**ARMAMENT:** two 7.7mm (0.303in) trainable forward-firing machine guns in nose turret, four 7.7mm (0.303in) trainable rearward-firing machine guns in tail turret and one 7.7mm (0.303in) trainable lateral-firing machine gun in each beam position, plus an internal bomb load of 2041kg (4500lb)

# Vought SB2U Vindicator

Ordered in October 1934, the SB2U was the US Navy's first monoplane scout and dive-bomber, although it is worth noting that lingering doubts about the monoplane's high take-off and landing speed meant that an order was also placed for a single XSB3U-1 biplane prototype. The XSB2U-1 monoplane prototype made its maiden flight in January 1936. In October of the same year, the US Navy ordered 54 SB2U-1 production aircraft with the 615kW (825hp) Pratt & Whitney R-1535-96 engine. The SB2U-1 was delivered from December 1937, after which followed 58 and 57 examples of the SB2U-2 with equipment changes and the SB2U-3 with heavier armament: and enlarged fuel tankage. The SB2U was phased out of service in 1942. France and the UK bought 39 and 50 generally similar V-156F and Chesapeake Mk I aircraft. Pictured is the SB2U-2 aircraft operated by the 5th section leader of Bombing Squadron VB-2 deployed on the USS *Lexington* in July 1939.

## SPECIFICATIONS

**COUNTRY OF ORIGIN:** United States
**TYPE:** (SB2U-3) two-seat carrierborne and land-based scout and dive-bomber
**POWERPLANT:** one 615kW (825hp) Pratt & Whitney R-1535-2 Twin Wasp Junior 14-cylinder two-row radial engine
**PERFORMANCE:** maximum speed 391km/h (243mph); initial climb rate 326m (1070ft) per minute; service ceiling 7195m (23,600ft); range 1802km (1120 miles)
**WEIGHTS:** empty 2556kg (5634lb); maximum take-off 4273kg (9421lb)
**WINGSPAN:** 12.77m (41ft 11in)
**LENGTH:** 10.36m (34ft)
**HEIGHT:** 4.34m (14ft 3in)
**ARMAMENT:** one 12.7mm (0.5in) fixed forward-firing machine gun in the port upper part of the forward fuselage and one 12.7mm (0.5in) machine gun in the rear cockpit, plus an external bomb load of 454kg (1000lb)

# Vultee A-35 Vengeance

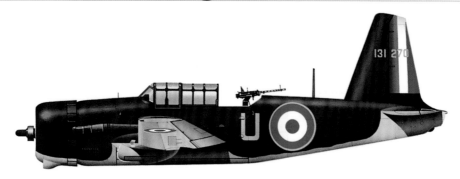

arly in 1940, Vultee received a French order for a dive-bomber and the contract stipulated the delivery of 300 of these V-72 aircraft by September 1941. France's fall brought a temporary halt to the programme, which was revived by British orders for 700 V-72 warplanes for service with the designations Vengeance Mks I and II. The US also bought 200 A-31 (Vengeance Mk III) aircraft for Lend-Lease transfer to the UK and then funded the A-35 with American equipment and greater wing incidence. The A-35 (100 aircraft) had the 1193kW (1600hp) R-2600-11 engine, the A-35A comprised 99 conversions with revised forward-firing armament and the A-35B (Vengeance Mk IV) comprised 563 further improved aircraft. Only limited operational use was made of the type, which was generally operated as a target tug. Pictured here is an A-35B Vengeance of Groupes de Bombardement 1/32, Free French Air Force, based in North Africa during 1943.

## SPECIFICATIONS

**COUNTRY OF ORIGIN:** United States
**TYPE:** (A-35B) two-seat dive-bomber and attack warplane
**POWERPLANT:** one 1267.5kW (1700hp) Wright R-2600-13 14-cylinder two-row radial engine
**PERFORMANCE:** maximum speed 449km/h (279mph); climb to 4570m (15,000ft) in 11 minutes 18 seconds; service ceiling 6795m (22,300ft); range 2253km (1400 miles)
**WEIGHTS:** empty 4672kg (10,300lb); maximum take-off 7439kg (16,400lb)
**WINGSPAN:** 14.63m (48ft)
**LENGTH:** 12.12m (39ft 9in)
**HEIGHT:** 4.67m (15ft 4in)
**ARMAMENT:** six 12.7mm (0.5in) fixed forward-firing machine guns in the leading edges of the wing and one 12.7mm (0.5in) trainable rearward-firing machine gun in the rear cockpit, plus an internal and external bomb load of 907kg (2000lb)

# Westland Wapiti

In the mid-1920s, the Royal Air Force began to appreciate the approaching 'block obsolescence' of its World War I-vintage de Havilland D.H.9A general-purpose biplane and issued a requirement for a replacement offering improved performance, greater load-carrying capability, a durable airframe capable of withstanding the rigours of operations in all the regions in which RAF had to fly and, most taxingly of all, maximum use of D.H.9A components of which the service had abundant stocks. The winning contender was the Westland Wapiti, which used the D.H.9A's wing cellule and tail unit. The Wapiti prototype first flew in March 1927 and, after some development, the type was built to the extent of 570 aircraft for the UK, Australia, Canada and South Africa in variants up to the Wapiti Mk VI and for China as the Wapiti Mk VIII. Pictured is a Mk IA of the Royal Australian Air Force, in service as a glider-tug during the 1940s.

## SPECIFICATIONS

**COUNTRY OF ORIGIN:** United Kingdom
**TYPE:** (Wapiti Mk III) two-seat general-purpose warplane
**POWERPLANT:** one 365kW (490hp) Armstrong Siddeley Jaguar VI 14-cylinder two-row radial engine
**PERFORMANCE:** maximum speed 225km/h (140mph); climb to 1525m (5000ft) in 4 minutes 18 seconds; service ceiling 6280m (20,600ft); range 1062km (660 miles)
**WEIGHTS:** empty 1442kg (3180lb); maximum take-off 2449kg (5400lb)
**WINGSPAN:** 14.15m (46ft 5in)
**LENGTH:** 9.91m (32ft 6in)
**HEIGHT:** 3.61m (11ft 10in)
**ARMAMENT:** one 7.7mm (0.303in) fixed forward-firing machine gun in the upper part of the forward fuselage and one 7.7mm (0.303in) trainable rearward-firing machine gun in the rear cockpit, plus an external bomb load of 263kg (580lb)

# Index